THE WILD WAY
To Lucid Dreaming

Waking.Induced.Lucid.Dreaming.

Lucid Dreaming On Demand!

By slider

Published by Lonebird Publications

© slider 2016
Reg No. 284700707

All rights reserved.
No part of this publication may be reproduced, stored in a retrieval system, or transmitted, in any form; electronic, mechanical, photocopying, recording, be lent, re-sold, hired out or otherwise circulated in any form of binding or cover other than that in which it is published, or by any means without the prior written permission of the author.

The opinions expressed herein are those of the author. The information in this book should not be treated as a substitute for medical advice. Any use of information in this book is at the reader's discretion and risk. The author cannot be held responsible for any loss, claim or damage arising out of the use, or misuse, of the suggestions made, or the failure to take medical advice on any of the issues raised.

Published by Lonebird Publications

ISBN 978-0-9935466-0-0

www.theWILDway.com
For more information and to visit
The WILD Way Forum

Contents

PREFACE 3

INTRODUCTION 5

    Learning to Lucid Dream 7

PART 1 – THEORY 9

    What is Lucid Dreaming? 11

    Why Learn to Lucid Dream? 23

    WILDs Versus DILDs 40

    History, Myths and Legends of Lucid Dreaming 46

PART 2 – PRACTICE 53

    Hypnagogia: The Key to WILDs 55

    Relaxation Techniques 62

    Entering the Lucid Dreaming State 72

- Levels of Lucidity 80
- Changing Dreams 87
- False Awakenings 92
- The Midway Point 95
- Lucid Dreaming on Demand 105

PART 3 – ADVANCED TECHNIQUES 109

- Additional Techniques for WILDs 111
- Techniques for DILDs 115
- The Philosophy of lucid dreaming 119
- Frequently Asked Questions 141

PART 4 – RESOURCES 149

- Recommended Reading 151
- Other Resources 152
- Glossary of Lucid Dreaming Terms 153

Acknowledgements 155

Hora Inmensa 159

About the Author

Slider (real name Brian Aherne) was born, and lives, in South London, England. *The WILD Way to Lucid Dreaming* is his debut publication.

Preface

For those of you who are completely new to lucid dreaming and would love to experience it, I say 'welcome'. You're definitely in the right place to find out exactly how to have incredible lucid dreams limited only by your own imagination. Thus, for anyone wanting to learn lucid dreaming, this book represents a one-stop-shop of everything you will ever need to know about the subject and how to learn to perfect this innate and unused ability we all have.

To others, who've already had some experience with lucid dreaming and who have probably been spending a small fortune trying out all the various available fancy techniques, (workshops, flashing face masks, ambient background music, self-hypnosis audio CDs, funky brainwave amplifiers and all the rest of it – laughs out loud) then all I can say to you is that you genuinely have my deepest respect if you have ever managed to have any lucid dreams using any of these methods. You can take comfort from the fact that the simple and straightforward technique outlined in this book is finally the answer to all your previous prayers, hopes, and yes, dreams too.

A simple method that ultimately translates into nothing less miraculous than the ability to lucid dream at will and, more importantly, on demand!

Need I say more? Then read on, and enjoy!

That said, and for the benefit of people completely new to the subject of lucid dreaming, the first part of this book will briefly outline the basic concept of what it actually is, and means, to experience lucid dreams. More experienced readers may wish to skip over this part in order to get straight down to business, but I recommend you read it anyway just to make sure that you've got it all completely correct, particularly if your whole effort to date has been based exclusively upon the 'dream-induced' version of lucid dreams only.

It only remains for me to wish you all rapid progress and great lucid dreams in the very near future. I would also like to wish you clarity in all that you undertake in this really quite phenomenal adventure.

Introduction

Learning to Lucid Dream

I struggled for years trying to use the traditional 'dream-initiated' method of lucid dreaming with, I might add, very little success and quite a lot of frustration. This was mainly because I seemed to spend more time thinking and planning lucid dreaming, than actually accomplishing it.

Anyway, I didn't set out to try other, alternative methods, rather it was a pure chance event that grew out of my sheer boredom of waiting for something (anything!) to happen using the usual Dream-Induced Lucid Dreaming (DILD) process, that led me to discover something that I only later learned was called Waking-Induced Lucid Dreaming (WILD).

Now for some reason totally unknown to me, between the two most basic methods of lucid dreaming available; 'Dream-Induced' and 'Waking-Induced', the WILD way is considered to be the more difficult of the two. Its practitioners are held in seemingly high esteem by those in dreaming circles who profess to be 'in-the-know', although I honestly don't know why, because experience has proven to me that the complete reverse is true.

For example, with DILDs one literally attempts to train oneself to fall asleep as per usual and to then wake up, later on, in an actual dream. An almost impossible thing to do! And yet, amazingly, people do manage to accomplish lucid dreaming in this manner, albeit with great difficulty and, in many cases, a growing sense of frustration. Not to mention having to put up in the meantime with all the mystique and cult-like mumbo-jumbo that typically surrounds the whole subject like an obscuring fog, mainly because absolutely nothing about DILDs is straightforward.

With WILDs, however, the complete opposite is true, in that with very little practice, one can learn to quite easily enter into a variety of lucid dreaming states, at will and on demand! Something that is much easier, makes sense, and involves no mystique or mumbo-jumbo whatsoever.

With WILDs, lucid dreaming becomes what it should be and needs to be; a thoroughly practical affair, in that you're rapidly learning to achieve consistently maximum lucidity in all lucid dreams, and far more importantly, having these lucid dreams only when you want to have them. I mean, who needs all the difficulty and ridiculous procedures of DILDs when you can just do it the WILD way instead? Big question, eh?

Lucid dreaming itself is incredibly easy to learn and do. Even though much of the teaching today on the subject relies solely on a complicated and complex training, one that increasingly involves expensive workshops and a variety of emerging audio-visual aids that are supposedly designed to somehow *unconsciously* induce one to lucid dream. (Good grief!)

The point, and clear aim of this book, however, is to bypass all the current rigmarole, pseudo-scientific paraphernalia and increasingly strange apparatus that tends to turn the whole thing into a rather expensive, awkward and uncomfortable, affair. Instead, I would like to put you in touch with a method of lucid dreaming that is not only very easy to put into practice, but one that will also provide you with rapid and startling results. A method that will cost you no further investment than the modest price of this book alone!

PART 1 – THEORY

What is Lucid Dreaming?

To date there have been many suggestions and convoluted explanations as to just what lucid dreaming might *actually* be and/or represent. These range all the way up from that of a mere meaningless glitch in our perceptual apparatus with the brain merely ticking over in standby mode while the body rests, to some extremely sophisticated shamanic practices that subsequently evolved to take advantage of some kind of deeper human psychic nature.

Technically speaking, however, especially in the context of a Waking-Induced Lucid Dream (WILD), as opposed to a Dream-Induced Lucid Dream (DILD) – lucid dreaming is ultimately no less than the ability to deliberately enter into an altered state of perceptual awareness in the full knowledge of doing so and remaining fully lucid for the duration.

Medical science suggests that ordinary dreaming is a purely natural phenomenon that all mammals exhibit, this being merely the result of random-type memories and neurons firing in our resting brain while the physical body sleeps. Moreover, they have also suggested that dreams are absolutely necessary to obtaining rest and that people deprived of having dreams altogether (dream deprivation as opposed to sleep deprivation) have been proven to be the worse for it, their physical health suffering as a result. So much so, that a person can even die as a direct result of not being allowed to have enough dreams and rapid eye movement (REM) sleep. This is because having these ordinary dreams might, in some indirect fashion, also allow us to work out any psychological problems and unresolved conflicts that we may be experiencing in our waking lives.

However convincing and glib that argument may be, this explanation doesn't totally account for the experiences many people have reported of occasionally becoming fully conscious and awake again whilst actually *having* a dream! A now acknowledged phenomenon called lucid dreaming, in order to distinguish it from the ordinary random dreams that everyone experiences. Lucid dreaming is generally considered to be something that scientists agree we shouldn't be able to do, but this is now beginning to be looked into again on the basis that it might just be associated with how our resulting sense of self is modelled.

It seems like a simple enough question doesn't it? But what lucid dreaming *actually* is could well turn out to be something far more reaching and revealing about our nature than just the obvious answer to this seemingly innocent enough question. That by digging around, in order to fully understand just what lucid dreaming really is, we may also have to re-examine what *ordinary* dreams and dreaming are too.

So, why then do we even dream at all? Moreover, is it really only as science suggests that our minds and brains are merely being minimally active even though we've gone to sleep? That because our brains don't quite shut down completely we then experience what everyone calls dreams? A reasonable enough argument, only, of course, this doesn't explain why it's then sometimes possible to become aware of being 'awake' in a dream. I mean, if our bodies are simply shutting down in order to rest and ordinary dreams are merely the result of random memories and neurons firing in our brain; then how can it be possible to regain full consciousness during such a shutdown of our entire physical and mental system? It's certainly very odd. So, maybe for lucid dreaming to be able to occur at all surely puts dreaming on another footing altogether, if not entirely. Right?

The most common form of this strange lucidity experienced during ordinary dreaming is the dream-induced version (DILD), which basically means to suddenly realise – right in the middle of a dream – that it is actually only a dream! The sudden jolt of realisation that one is, in fact, dreaming being something that can, and does, quite easily bounce an inexperienced dreamer right back out of the dreaming state to full waking. That is, unless certain precautions and modifications to one's behaviour are learned and adopted beforehand in order to compensate for the very natural emotional reaction to such waking, a 'yikes' effect that all newbies to lucid dreaming will quite naturally initially experience upon realising that they are suddenly awake and conscious in a dream-state scenario.

What lucid dreaming *actually* is, however, or may ultimately represent in people's lives, might just be another matter altogether, possibly a far more complicated and altogether philosophical one. The answer to which, if we could find it, would possibly not only explain *why* such a thing as lucid dreaming can occur, but also might indirectly provide us with more definitive answers to the age-old question as to why we all have to fall sleep and have dreams in the first place. Everyone dreams! Even animals have dreams! And many rational and logical scientists have only ever proposed rather clinical ideas about what dreaming actually is and why there seems to be some physiological and psychological need to them lest we become both physically and psychologically unhealthy. Exactly what dreaming really is though has so far been something that scientists and dream researchers alike haven't managed to nail down beyond talking about alpha and beta waves, neurons randomly firing in the brain, plus lots of squiggles on long rolling EEC charts.

The hard fact of the matter is that we all dream. And to date, no one really knows just what sleep and dreaming really are or why we all have to do it. Sleep and dreaming being something everyone experiences from the moment of birth; it seems to be just another part of life that everyone has come to unquestionably accept. Falling asleep and having dreams is such a regular event in everyone's lives, and the lives of most of the creatures on this planet, it has become second nature to just go along with it and let it happen. It is so normal, in fact, that we even have different categories of sleep ranging from catnaps, through several hours of restful sleep that includes periods of ordinary dreaming, to the sleep of the completely exhausted who have stayed awake for longer than normal and then fall into a deep sleep for anything up to thirty-six hours depending on just how sleep deprived they'd become!

Accordingly, and throughout history, there have been a great many claims and myths in one form or another attributed to our having dreams. These range from the flying sorcerers of the South Americas, to witches riding on their broomsticks in the west, to the Dreamtime of the Australian Aborigines. Stories and myths abound. From Freud to Einstein, claims have also been made as to dreams having potentially deeper, hidden significance in our lives. Even so, dreaming remains, for the most part, something of an enigma that people generally don't pay much attention to on a daily basis beyond maybe commenting on particularly pleasant or weird examples. Dreams are curious experiences sometimes, but as far as most people are concerned that's just about all there seems to be to it. End of story!

However, what if you could dream in such a way that all the time you'd normally spend fast asleep was instead filled with stimulating and amazing experiences that you would otherwise like to do during the day, perhaps even more so? Consider, for example, going to visit another country or a famous landmark that you've always wanted to see or, perhaps, standing on the top of Mount Everest to look at the amazing view. Or even flying through the air like a bird! Because with lucid dreaming the sky is the limit. And although it may not be the actual Mount Everest that you are standing on in a dream, while you're there it still seems about as real as anything can be. Only, at the same time, you also know that it's all just a dream. You could, for example, jump (or even fall) all the way from the top to the bottom of a 'dream' Mount Everest and never be harmed so it's also completely safe.

There are also those who claim that it is possible to visit real places in dreaming; so-called astral projection and out of the body experiences. But for now I only wish to examine having standard lucid dreams and of being able, during the hours of sleep, to wander around and explore what seems to be another world (or even a series of them) instead of merely wasting that time snoring away the downtime of our ordinary, random and mostly forgotten dreams.

An interesting and notable fact about lucid dreaming is the really wonderful and incredible afterglow from having experienced one. This is something that anyone who has ever experienced lucid dreaming will attest to, along with the seemingly energising effect of the post lucid dreaming experience. And although just about any stimulating experience produces similarly wonderful feelings of emotional uplift and exhilaration, sometimes for hours afterwards, nothing seems to beat the sheer adrenalin-rush (if that's what it really is) that lucid dreaming produces. A sensation that can linger not just for hours afterwards, but for days. Something I suspect that doesn't actually have anything to do with adrenalin as such and is probably more to do with some kind of spiritual-cum-energetic refreshment (if there really is such a thing), resulting in an unusually deep kind of satisfaction and inner-peace. Or maybe it could be better described as experiencing terrifically warm feelings of utter confidence, coupled with an unshakable inner calm and overall sense of well-being. It's hard to describe but is nonetheless quite an unmistakable sensation. One you'll very quickly learn to recognise as the mark of having genuine lucid dreams.

For example, for days after my first real lucid dreaming experience I didn't feel tired at all and everything seemed much brighter and sharper than ever before. Everywhere I looked quite ordinary and commonplace objects were suddenly all far more interesting than they would otherwise normally have been. Colours were somehow enhanced and more vibrant and I found myself staring at everything with undeniable interest, almost as if I were seeing all these quite ordinary things for the first time. Reds and greens particularly were somehow more intense than I had ever remembered seeing them. Textures too were all enhanced to the eye.

For instance, I remember walking past a wall that I must have passed a hundred times or more previously on my way to and from the local shops and had never really paid much attention to. After all, a wall is just a wall, right? Yet this time something about the way that wall looked made me pause to wonder just what exactly was different about it this time. For sure it was still only a wall, but the texture of its yellowish bricks all seemed different somehow, all better or warmer in some way. The fine details and tiny pockmarks in the bricks' surfaces appeared clearer and more defined than I ever remembered having seen them. I can even say that they were attractive in some strange but pleasing way because they were anything except ordinary anymore. I must have stared at and examined that wall for nigh on fifteen minutes, initially caring little about the looks I was starting to get from passers-by. I could feel people looking at me and wondering if I was alright, which is what anyone would probably think if they saw someone staring at a wall. But, quite unusually for me at that time, I didn't care what other people thought of me. I ran my fingers over the surfaces of the wall many times just feeling all the tiny little bumps and indentations in it, thoroughly enjoying the novel sensations coming to me and only reluctantly tearing myself away from it because of the overt attention I was starting to attract. Subjectively, it was as though something had happened to my eyes to improve their sight several fold. And not only my eyes but all my other senses as well! I was really enjoying myself and everything around me now seemed to hold some new fascination. Something in me had noticeably changed and somehow all for the better. An unfamiliar inner certainty assured me that all was well and that I had absolutely nothing to worry about. This was the only thing that did slightly worry me as I was not generally given to such strong feelings of confidence. But apart from that, I felt great!

The point of relating this experience to you is to explain the suspicion on my part, then and now, of what appears to be some kind of unfamiliar boost in energy that resulted in all my senses being somehow subjectively enhanced. For days after my first real lucid dreaming experience I was literally hopping about and giggling, making jokes and laughing in ways I hadn't since childhood. For the first time in ages, I was thoroughly enjoying myself. My feelings of solid good health and inner well-being seemed to be at an all-time high and I loved it. But I could also sense a direct correlation between having lucid dreamed and the appearance of this new and wonderful energetic state of being, which, for days afterwards, was just bubbling up from inside of me without any effort on my part.

It felt as though I'd just had the best night's sleep of my life, even though I hadn't slept at all and had, in fact, spent the entire five hours of the experience quite consciously crossing back and forth between that of waking and lucid dreaming. My suspicion today, after many similar experiences, is that the natural refreshment of ordinary sleep had somehow been mightily enhanced by my having lucid dreams instead of falling asleep as usual and just having ordinary non-lucid ones. In other words; the experience itself tends to suggest that the merest contact with the dream state is enough to refresh us energetically rather than that refreshment being simply the result of having physically rested and the standard assumption that falling asleep is merely the result of feeling tired and of the need to rest after the day's activities. Only I'm beginning to think that this is not quite the full story of what's really going on when we sleep.

For instance, how about if what's really occurring is that when we've used up most of our energy during the course of the day in maintaining waking consciousness, that energy quite naturally begins to wane and the only way to replenish it is by entering into a dreaming state. That what *really* refreshes us is not the physically resting part of sleep so much as having dreams! Something which might also account for why people, when allowed to sleep but being deprived of having the REM-type dreams associated with them, eventually become so weak that they wither away and die. In other words, what we normally call 'getting tired' and 'feeling sleepy' might just be the beginnings of an *involuntary* entering into an altered state of awareness whereby we can then dream in order to refresh our waning energy supply. The fact that we generally enter into that altered state completely unconsciously in a process that we've all learned to recognise as 'falling asleep', being what ultimately gives rise to experiencing ordinary 'non-lucid' dreams, when what's really happening to us is that we're being pulled into an altered state of awareness against our will.

This 'falling asleep' has subsequently turned into the standard and unquestioned routine we've learned to call bedtime. The point is that to go against routine and enter *deliberately* into a dreaming state has an inordinate effect upon our energy supply, to the extent that, not only does a person receive an extra boost in terms of refreshment, but also requires far less contact with dreaming, or even sleeping, in order to do so. In which case what lucid dreaming *really* is, is nothing less than the 'conscious' returning to an energising state of awareness from which we can then top up our dwindling energy supply. Something which quite naturally becomes depleted from the prolonged effort of maintaining normal waking awareness for long periods of time!

For example, as a new father at the age of twenty-four it was explained to me by an attending nurse that very young babies always fall asleep right after nursing. Not so much because their meal makes them feel sleepy but because young infants apparently don't yet have *enough* energy to remain both awake and grow at the same time! The implication being that maintaining a waking awareness is actually quite costly in terms of the energy expended. Too costly, in fact, for a very young infant who needs all its energy just to grow during what is an energetically critical time in its life. In reality, infants only really wake up to feed and then go right back to sleep purely in order to digest that food and grow. Only later, as they get older and start to accumulate more energy in their growing size and mass, do they gradually become enabled to remain awake for increasingly longer periods of time. The point being, that because there is no premium on our having dreams, we have all established an unconscious habit whereby all of our awareness is routinely focused solely upon the waking state alone. The result for an adult being an approximate sixteen hour day of waking awareness followed by around eight hours of sleep, only some of which is actually spent in REM dreams. This seems perfectly natural and absolutely normal to people if only because we've spent our entire lifetime to date doing so!

But what if there was an alternative to this, a far more conscious and aware one? One whereby a person deliberately entered consciously and fully aware into the dreaming state in order to re-energise themselves instead of allowing themselves to be unconsciously pulled into sleep by dint of having used up all their available energy in prolonged waking activities. Would that not make some kind of a difference, not only to the way people choose to live but also in terms of how we view ourselves? I think it would, because not only would one potentially require less sleep than before, and as such be able to effectively extend one's waking activities to more than that of sixteen hours on average, but it might also have repercussions on the amount of food needed in order to supplement our daily waking requirements as well.

Moreover, the usual view we have of ourselves would have to change to incorporate the understanding that there is probably quite a bit more to our awareness than possibly meets the eye. Especially if our innate ability to lucid dream becomes an important, if not intrinsic, part of it. I mean, how might we be forced to view ourselves if lucid dreaming became the norm instead of remaining an unusual pastime practised only by the few; wouldn't that tend to make quite a big difference in how we all see ourselves in our daily lives?

Personally, I think it would change our view of ourselves inordinately. That, far from being just another pastime that people can learn to amuse themselves with occasionally and then make nothing more of, lucid dreaming could, under such circumstances, become as much a genuinely serious daily activity as going to work or eating our dinner. The rather tidy, not to mention dull, acceptance of a daily, almost completely unconscious *downtime* required in order to rest would have to be amended to include perhaps not only shorter periods of rest but also the striking realisation that consciously entering into the dreaming state is crucial to our state of well-being in terms of the energy one obtains from doing so.

Given the choice, most people would, I'm sure, almost certainly opt for a shorter period of rest coupled with a boost in terms of energy, one that also seemingly enhances and enriches their waking senses too. Accordingly, by dint of being awake in our dreams, our so-called daily downtime of ordinary sleep and dreaming would almost certainly become a thing of the past. Instead, ordinary sleep would become something that only very young people still experienced while they had yet to enter more consciously into the dreaming state in order to energise themselves. Perhaps there would eventually even have to be classes for young people reaching a certain age in order for them to begin to learn to control their awareness more accurately and acutely during the hours of so-called sleep, the mastering of which would become another rite of passage that all would pass through on their way to adulthood. Just how this curriculum would be taught, however, remains unknown until such times as a wider acceptance of the importance of our ability to lucid dream actually comes to pass.

So what is lucid dreaming? For the time being, and until such time as the whole edifice of dreaming, and that of lucid dreaming in particular, has been more thoroughly investigated and understood; lucid dreaming can simply be looked upon as being the technique whereby ordinary dreams are turned into a far more conscious activity. One that is not only highly enjoyable and stimulating, but also increases one's general level of awareness, perception and feelings of health and well-being.

Is all this perhaps just a little too far-fetched for you to accept? Well, they laughed at Jules Verne[1] too, didn't they?

---

[1] 19th century French writer renowned for his influence on the literary world and, in particular science fiction.

Why Learn to Lucid Dream?

Assuming you have already attained a certain degree of proficiency in the ability to lucid dream, a number of questions quite naturally begin to arise about exactly what uses and applications this newly developed ability could be applied to. The question being: what is lucid dreaming good for?

Well, there are many reasons why people might like to learn to lucid dream. Here perhaps are some of the better known ones:

Entertainment value

Believe me, if you've never done it before, there is nothing more entertaining or exciting than finding oneself fully awake and conscious in a lucid dreaming situation, where the only limit to what you want to do next is your own imagination! For, in lucid dreaming even the sky is no longer the limit in that journeys into a virtual form of outer space are also entirely conceivable. Visiting places like the Moon, for example, being literally no more than a thought away! In dreams, apparently, anything is possible and zooming around in a virtual outer space is actually really no more outlandish than flying around in an equally virtual sky is back here on Earth. The facility for travelling in the dream state being enhanced beyond measure, makes distance no object, or even relevant, come to that. If you'd like to open a window in your life onto endless adventure and excitement then lucid dreaming is definitely for you.

Exploring the unknown

I can't speak for anyone else, but from observation it appears that in the initial stages of learning to lucid dream, travelling to unknown places is far more likely than visiting more familiar landmarks. This means that, from the point of view of lucid dreaming, visiting the unknown is the default value. And that consequently, nine times out of ten, you'll find yourself, at least initially, in a strange locale albeit surrounded by thoroughly familiar objects, almost as though you were visiting a foreign land. Things appear more or less the same only different. Of course, with increased experience comes the ability to go more where you'd like to go and see what you'd like to see. Known tourist locations such as the Pyramids of Giza for example, or the Eiffel Tower in Paris, present little difficulty.

However, there is always something hauntingly beautiful about the unknown which seems to have a quality all its own. One in which the spirit of adventure looms noticeably larger than life. Almost as if the unknown by itself invites one to dare to travel into, and across, its boundaries. Even to the point of supplying you with the required sense of adventure and daring in order to do so. With practice, pretty much anything is possible in a lucid dream, including visiting virtual landmarks both known and unknown.

To experience flying

You'll quickly find out for yourself that in lucid dreaming flying is a given. For some unknown reason, to fly in dreaming is as normal and as second nature as walking is in waking awareness. Just why this should be so I really can't say other than to state that it is, as with so many other things. In dreaming some things just 'are' with no rational explanation for them. I guess flying has to be my personal favourite and I can honestly tell you there's nothing quite the same as soaring like a bird through the air to utterly banish all lingering doubts and thoughts from one's awareness. The resulting overwhelming sense of unparalleled freedom is indescribable! So wonderful, in fact, that I'm reluctant to analyse it beyond enjoying the experience itself for fear of somehow maybe taking something away from it for myself.

The best thing to do, of course, is simply to experience it for yourself in your very first lucid dream just by holding the intention to fly just as soon as you realise that you're in a lucid dreaming situation. I even recommend it because, not only does flying in a lucid dream instantly remove any final vestiges of rational doubt from your mind, it also prolongs the dreaming experience by distracting one from the initially unavoidable emotional reaction of being in an unfamiliar situation, somewhat like a rabbit transfixed by the headlights of an approaching car might feel. Although the outcome in this instance differs considerably in that, instead of getting run over like the unfortunate rabbit, in lucid dreaming one simply (and rather frustratingly) finds oneself instantly awake in bed and no longer dreaming; the 'D'oh! factor' (to quote Homer Simpson!).

I guess I could easily wax lyrical about flying in lucid dreams for possibly several chapters and still not be tired of the subject and, even then, not really begin to convey to you just exactly what it's like to do so. So I'll spare you that and suggest it is suffice to say that flying in dreaming is probably going to be one of the greatest and most fulfilling experiences you'll ever have. So all I can really add is 'enjoy'!

Extra mobility

There is something utterly refreshing and invigorating about moving around in lucid dreams. Whether one walks, runs, or more simply, flies and zooms about, the very act of moving seems to put one immediately in touch with a greater sense of inner being or self, almost as though that was the most comfortable and comforting thing in the world. There is a definite exhilaration factor involved, a unique sense of liberation and/or abandon as though one is suddenly released after many years from a restricting cage. In many ways, this is probably not that far from the truth because, once free, one's spirit literally soars with an indescribable joy in some kind of fundamental and restoring way. It's also a feeling that is carried back into the waking world that can last for several days afterwards. Not all may be going well for you back in the waking world, but after lucid dreaming one's inner spirit feels more connected and alive. I can thoroughly recommend it!

It's a sad fact in life that many people are, unfortunately, physically challenged in various ways, some maybe permanently confined to a wheelchair either from birth, through illness or accident, many of whom would perhaps love to be able to move about again in ways they've either not been able to for a long time, or indeed were never able to. In my opinion lucid dreaming could well be useful to such people, both mentally and emotionally, possibly even physically too, in the sense that feeling really good in oneself (a seemingly automatic benefit of having lucid dreams) can be a powerfully motivating factor that encourages people to try to do more for themselves in all things. The boost of self-esteem and confidence, plus the feeling of connectedness to everything around you that is automatically engendered by just the act of lucid dreaming alone, can certainly be an invaluable resource of hidden strength and fortitude in the face of adversity.

And, if lucid dreaming can provide incredible sensations of freedom and liberation in people who do not have a disability, that might also be the case for the physically challenged? Therefore, it strikes me that it might just be a possible for handicapped or immobile people to be able to experience a sense of physical freedom and mobility that they would otherwise find impossible. People who suddenly find themselves confined to a wheelchair could, for example, perhaps again experience the simple pleasure of going for a walk, a run or even a swim, something which under normal circumstances may not be possible. Also, taking into consideration the highly uplifting effects of having lucid dreamed, in some cases it might even help to alleviate depression!

Cognitive therapy

The old adage of people having to face their fears in order to overcome them definitely seems to contain a measure of truth, because for those suffering from them, phobias are no joking matter. Life is difficult enough, is it not, without having a phobia of any description to complicate things further? The restrictions that having a phobia can place upon a person's activities ranges from being mildly annoying to completely incapacitating. The recommended treatment for such ailments is often of alternative or cognitive therapy, the aim of which is to alter the way a person responds and reacts to particular criteria and situation. The person in question, presumably, gradually gains control over their own, sometimes severe, emotional reactions by a process of an increasing familiarity with the object of their fears. The more often someone encounters the very thing that has been worrying them, the less it begins to affect them, until in the end the object of their overreaction becomes what it really was all along; just another thing to deal with and no better or worse than anything else by comparison.

The root cause of this overreaction is the over-emphasis (for whatever reason initially) of that one particular item or idea over any other, until one's emotions take on a life of their own in terms of reacting increasingly violently to it. It comes as no surprise to me, therefore, when I hear that some people are apparently having success at using the safety of the lucid dreaming situation to practice dealing with things that they'd otherwise run a mile from in waking awareness. The agoraphobic, for instance, having the courage to venture outside within the safe confines of a lucid dream, knowing that it is only a dream. Similarly, people scared of heights or of going on aeroplanes may benefit from facing their fears, because lucid dreaming provides them with a virtual and safe means of doing so.

Let me put it another way; even indirectly lucid dreaming is automatically conducive to overcoming obsessions and phobias because, in order to prolong and maintain a lucid dream, one is forced to learn to deal with everything one encounters slightly differently from normal, and curbing one's usual emotional and mental reactions to average situations is one of them. The practice of lucid dreaming thus tends to re-examine what are otherwise taken for granted items and ideas in a manner conducive, and similar to, that which cognitive therapy sets out to achieve. Moreover, allowing such severe reactions to things in dreaming inevitably results in being immediately booted out of the dream state. From the very beginning the whole goal and automatic thrust of the novice in dreaming is to curb any such reactions merely in order to maintain their lucid dreaming scenarios. Something which is so exciting and stimulating that the drive to prolong the experience becomes paramount, thus providing a powerful incentive to persevere as the rewards are so great. Perhaps even actors suffering from stage-fright could possibly learn to rehearse their lines and roles by creating the dream scenario of being in an audience-filled theatre until they feel completely confident of their ability to perform in front of them. At least I don't see why not. The potentially useful therapeutic applications of lucid dreaming are nigh on endless assuming even a modicum of the lucid dreaming ability that WILDs ultimately provides.

Self-healing

Visualisation techniques used in medicine to promote rapid healing are generally more accepted now than they used to be. Not that long ago, you would have been laughed at and scorned if you even suggested such a thing! Yet it turns out that the so-called 'placebo effect' can indeed be a force for good in human beings when it comes to rallying the body's own defences and its own ability to heal itself under certain conditions. If this is so, where better to practice those techniques than in lucid dreaming?

Inner development

If developing one's inner being is a euphemism for getting closer to one's inner self and, perhaps, being more in contact with reality, then I'd say that, lucid dreaming develops one's inner being by giving it some of the exercise it so badly needs in order to stretch its wings and grow. The term 'spiritual exercise' is too vague and generalised to be of much practical use to anyone, but I guess lucid dreaming could certainly fall in that category together with other practices like meditation and yoga, especially if one were to consider lucid dreaming to be part of one's meditations and the inner experience gained from such practices. The simple truth is that, the more one comes in contact with one's own inner being the more it becomes available to you. And nothing places you in direct contact with one's inner self more than lucid dreaming! Of course, meditation and yoga have a similar effect, although nothing is as compelling and encouraging as lucid dreaming by comparison. I mean, a dedicated and disciplined person could meditate for years and hardly see any noticeable effects beyond, perhaps, the gradual slow strengthening of their inner character and balanced sense of peace. Like anything really, it takes discipline to perform meditation every day until it eventually begins to count. Whereas, with lucid dreaming the results are not only virtually instantaneous but also absolutely staggering as well. The only discipline involved (which is actually quite similar to meditation) is to maintain the correct state of mind that prolongs the experience, something which, of course, takes a little while to learn, but within a very short period of time it becomes increasingly easy to lucid dream almost at will.

This 'lucid dreaming on demand' is key to mastering a more general awareness of how perception actually functions and works in real time, waking awareness, as well as in dreaming, basically because the inner cognitive apparatus of perception employed in both instances are literally one and the same. Thus, whatever your particular purpose is in learning to do it, be prepared, as your proficiency increases, for lucid dreaming to eventually begin to have potentially far-reaching effects in your daily waking world and your personal outlook on life in general. Why? Because at the very basic level there would seem to be two main areas to this lucid dreaming business which you'll quickly discover.

Firstly, the very personal, and potentially completely self-indulgent, aspect of the whole thing, one in which any of your strangest and wildest fantasies can easily and quickly be made to come true, albeit it only virtually. A kind of voyeurs' utopia and personal virtual reality entertainment-centre (think 'Holodeck' of *Star Trek* fame) all rolled into one! Secondly, a somewhat more sober and objective approach where one explores the dreaming state as an explorer and observer only. The better perhaps to record events as they unfold more accurately, possibly with a view to mapping some of the confines of the near unknown, not only for your own greater understanding of it for yourself, but also for the benefit of others if you were inclined to consider sharing that information.

Without that objectivity there is also the possibility that, because lucid dreaming is a completely subjective state of being that's directly connected to one's inner sense of reality, the dreams themselves can therefore come to mean whatever you might personally want them to mean depending on what you happen to believe in. Thus, a word of caution is recommended in this direction. That if, for example, you are a very religious person your lucid dreams might very easily begin to automatically adopt religious-type connotations. The only problem there being that if you go looking for 'God' (or angels or whatever) then for sure you'll probably find 'something', only in reality it's unlikely to *be* God or a real angel. A friend of mine, for example, upon finding himself in a lucid dream asked to know what God was, and to his utter surprise was presented with an image of himself looking young and healthy, dressed in a pure white suit. He certainly wasn't expecting that! What this image actually represented perplexed him in the extreme. Nor did he ever find out beyond the occasional wry comment from his friends about what a psychologist would probably make of it all. So all in all, it's probably better not to be tempted to try finding such things, leastways without knowing for sure before you do so that the answers (if any) will probably be rather cryptic to say the least.

Moreover, there are other, similar, things that one could easily become quite lost in if it's not consciously guarded against. This kind of thing (going into lucid dreaming with a prior agenda, I mean) being one of the main reasons why I'd personally recommend choosing the second option and attempting to remain as objective as possible about the whole dreaming experience and thereby behaving accordingly as one's experience and knowledge of the lucid dreaming state expands. Otherwise, just what you do or don't do with lucid dreaming is of course left entirely to yourself, the dreamer, and to your own personal codes of conduct and conscience.

Rehearsing events

I've just been reading about people who use lucid dreaming to rehearse upcoming events, such as a speech they are planning to give. All I can say to that is, WOW! What a stupendous idea! The whole thing of course hinges solely upon being able to repeat the experience enough times in dreaming to be of any real value. This definitely applies to WILDs rather than DILDs.

There are just so many things that can (or could) be rehearsed ahead of time. Interviews and appointments of all kinds! Dance routines! Live performances of any description! Exams! The list is virtually endless and the sky the limit!

Problem solving

Finding novel solutions to common problems is legendary, both in ordinary dreams and in lucid dreaming. A person becomes so obsessed with a problem that it carries over into their subconscious mind and they eventually dream about it, in the process they sometimes even discover a brilliant and novel answer to whatever was on their mind. Too many reputable people attest to having had this experience for it to be discounted as a mere coincidence or a fluke, a phenomenon that is then enhanced a hundred-fold when applied to lucid dreaming due to this ability to repeat the experience at will.

To obtain such answers in *ordinary* dreams one might have to spend many days, or even weeks, deeply pondering a question in the waking world (as Einstein apparently did) before it then carries over into one's dreams to be answered, if it ever does, that is. On the other hand, with lucid dreaming, particularly with the WILDs version, full memories from the waking world are more usually always available to a higher degree, and your question can be voiced the very next time you are dreaming instead of having to wait on chance to provide the opportunity. In other words, if you accept the premise that answers to daily problems can sometimes be found in our dreams, then, logically speaking, lucid dreaming is the perfect place to seek these answers and discover whether the process is viable. Artists, for example, might well find something in lucid dreaming to inspire them to paint, and writers may well dissolve their writer's block by seeing new options or resolutions to problems they'd never even consciously considered. There's no doubt about it, lucid dreaming is literally a goldmine in terms of all things creative. If Albert Einstein could find answers to incredibly complex equations in dreaming, then finding simple answers to more common problems should be much easier! Lucid dreaming provides a form of indirect access to the subconscious mind and memories, and there is seemingly no limit to what could be achieved if people just make the effort.

Sex

Basically, everyone makes mistakes at first ha! For most people the experience of suddenly starting to have lucid dreams can prove overwhelming, particularly for men, in that it can all quickly become just another avenue to find and have as much sex as they possibly can. Not that there's anything wrong in having sex you understand, real or otherwise, only that once the habit of doing so becomes established in lucid dreaming, it can become very difficult after that to alter one's agenda to do anything else. Something which, I suppose, is fine if that is all your imagination can aspire to. Only, of course, one also has to realise that there might just be much more to life, the universe and everything than the sexual act alone. In other words, by all means use lucid dreaming to have sex a few times, if you really have to, just don't make a habit of it or you'll quickly find that lucid dreaming, and the whole purpose for doing it, soon becomes about very little else!

For example, someone I know who has been lucid dreaming for years, regularly uses lucid dreaming to go prowling for sexual encounters, even though he's actually a happily married man of many years. Some of the stories he's related to me about his sexual dream exploits have, however, been really hilarious on occasion. I'm pretty sure he doesn't tell his wife about them lest who knows what she might think of him. On the other hand, maybe she knows him all too well and is glad that he confines his regular cheating and philandering to the world of lucid dreaming instead of doing something similar out in the waking world. One can only hope, for her sake anyway, that he does indeed confine himself in such a way. The point here is that, from talking to him, I know he knows better than that really. Yet he has let the main goal of his lucid dreaming experiences become the finding of, and having, sexual adventures and very little else. By all accounts he also really likes to fly in his lucid dreaming, but from what he says that's just about all he can be bothered to do with it these days. This strikes me as being a bit of a shame considering all the things that *can* be done with it. This is something that I've joked and jibed him about for years, until one day, having a joke back with me, he rather laughingly announced that, "Aw shucks, I hardly ever shag anyone in my dreams these days!" A remark which, at the time, I remember sent me into convulsions of giggles, a real 'coffee-spurt' moment, which still makes me laugh to this day just remembering it.

This isn't really a moral tirade on my part, only that obviously there is more to life, and consequently to lucid dreaming, than gratuitous sexual indulgence. Ultimately, though, everyone will simply have to decide for themselves what exactly they're going to do, or not do, with it all – versus, the very real temptation to use lucid dreaming for self-indulgence alone. All of which I feel comes more under the heading of entertainment rather than any kind of genuine exploration into what life, the universe and everything is all about. The latter being a much more sobering subject, which I fully realise might not be to everyone's liking or taste, especially to the young and frisky to whom lucid dreaming could so easily become just another means of indulging their appetites instead of going any further with it, and discovering what the opportunity of being *able* to lucid dream might ultimately represent.

Be assured, it's really very strange, standing there in some dream scenario of a room looking at the walls and the floor and at everything in there where everything seems quite real and normal, even to the touch. Except that you also know beyond the shadow of a doubt that all of this seeming reality is only a dream. And just to prove it to yourself you might gently levitate into the air with just the mere thought of doing so. Suddenly, one is filled with a feeling of energy and exhilaration. An overall mood of adventure and the joy of discovery floods and pervades your entire being, which literally tingles with excitement. All this accompanied by an unparalleled sensation of utter, unrestricted freedom!

Why learn to lucid dream? Because, for starters, it's an incredibly exhilarating and mind-blowing experience. Think about it! Lucid dreaming is being fully conscious and awake... in your dreams! Something which, I believe, directly or indirectly, can also be the beginning of a deeper inquiry into the, as yet, undiscovered nature of our human psyche.

The point is that one quite naturally begins, at some point along the line of lucid dream exploration, to wonder just how and why such a thing as lucid dreaming can even occur in the first place. Ordinary dreams, yes, but why 'lucid' dreaming exactly? (Something I'll go into more later.) Moreover, for anyone who is regularly awake in a dream, eventually the question automatically arises of how it's even possible to be doing this. The question is: just what is it about our mind that has this incredible ability to project itself into a three-dimensional virtual reality that's seemingly as real and as convincing as the waking world, sometimes even more so?

Objectively speaking, the only real reason to explore lucid dreaming is to discover hidden aspects of ourselves, where it all possibly leads or points to, and/or to discover just what it is about the mind that allows such things as virtual realities, that we can project, inhabit and explore for prolonged periods of time, to exist.

Another thing I can tell you about lucid dreaming is that the steady practice of it also eventually causes one to begin re-evaluating one's own life and life circumstances, in that most people have unwittingly allowed themselves to become almost completely caught up in their workplace and homes, their families and hobbies. So much so, that there remains very little room left in their lives with which to explore any of the deeper, perhaps hidden, meanings of life. Most people are so busy and involved in their current activities that they simply haven't got the time left over to explore anything more meaningful, even if it is available to them. In which case, learning to activate their innate ability to lucid dream can also offer people a kind of second chance at this, so to speak, and to take a look at opportunities to do so they may have inadvertently missed.

The fact is that the intelligent and observational approach to lucid dreaming eventually begins to carry-over into a person's waking awareness as well, thus presenting them with countless new opportunities to tweak the often rigidly fixed values of their waking life in a variety of ways. A chance they wouldn't otherwise get under any other circumstances, at least not until they were very much older, possibly even retired, and had the spare time in their lives to even consider looking at everything again.

The truth being, that it is probably better for someone to re-evaluate their life situation while they are still young rather than waiting until they have fulfilled all or most of their duties to their families, friends and work in society, before finding themselves with enough free time to be able to re-examine their lives and the way they live to any meaningful degree.

So, why learn to lucid dream? Well, possibly because it might just present a person with what is ultimately the opportunity of a lifetime; a genuine chance to totally re-examine their life and the way they're living it. And thus an opportunity they might never otherwise get to enrich their lives beyond measure in terms of the boost to the 'quality' of life they will very likely experience from that re-examination. If all you are looking for is cheap thrills then learning to lucid dream will almost certainly help you to fulfil that goal in virtually any form you can possibly imagine. Although, I personally would tend to consider that purpose to be an unworthy one, an opportunity missed to do more than just adding to your quota of amusements. Lucid dreaming isn't really just another games console to add to the growing number of entertainment centres that people avail themselves of to pass the time. Although, of course, it can indeed be employed as such if that was all someone was interested in.

Lucid dreaming changes your life! I mean, yes, it can be used solely for the purpose of entertainment and treated as if it's just another day out in some amazing theme park, only there might also be a lot more to the world of lucid dreaming and the opportunities it offers than these amusement aspects alone.

I guess, in the end, everyone has to decide for themselves what lucid dreaming might personally mean to them and for them. Especially from the DILDs point of view wherein full lucidity and full waking memory of who you are and what you are supposed to be doing isn't always as readily available to the dreamer as it is from the WILDs point of view wherein one generally has access to full lucidity and waking memories. In fact, this is the only real problem with DILDs, in that *dream-initiated* lucid dreaming automatically plunges the dreamer into a deeper level of dreaming than he is likely to be able to cope with. This is particularly so in the initial stages where the lack of access to full waking memories during a DILD has the tendency to bemuse the dreamer and cloud his judgement, to the extent that he becomes involuntarily more involved in the images of his dreams than he would otherwise probably want to.

There are many, many reasons why learning to lucid dream could be interesting, the best of which (as it was for me at any rate) is the clear sense of a continually expanding awareness and not just of oneself, but also of the world around you. In my opinion there is no end to the potentially unrealised useful applications of lucid dreaming that only await discovery by experienced and inexperienced practitioners alike.

To be fully conscious and aware in a dreaming state, and to be able to repeat that experience at will and on demand, is no less than the equivalent of the opening and exploration of an entirely new frontier.

WILDs Versus DILDs

Whatever lucid dreaming actually is it seems to fall into two distinct categories, the first being much better known and written about than the second. The first is the currently more traditional and better publicised Dream-Induced Lucid Dreaming (DILD).This method of lucid dreaming involves training oneself to regain waking consciousness whilst already in the middle of a regular dream – a nearly impossible thing to do!

The second method, however, is the lesser known Waking-Induced Lucid Dreaming (WILD), a simpler and far more direct approach that involves entering into lucid dreaming directly without having to first fall asleep and have regular dreams. The WILD method is what this book will be primarily concerned with exploring and helping you to put into practice.

Picture this; at a time of your own choosing you make yourself comfortable, laying down in bed or stretching out on a couch, and, after only a few minutes of getting yourself 'in the zone', you then step boldly into an incredibly lucid dream that is just as real to you as the waking world. Possibly, even more so because now you can do quite a few extra really amazing things like soaring right up into the air like Superman, or Neo in *The Matrix*, because with WILDs you can lucid dream as little or as much as you wish. This represents a genuine revolution in lucid dreaming as it is currently understood, since WILDS is effectively nothing less than 'lucid dreaming on demand'!

The problem with DILDs is the need to repeatedly practice increasingly exotic techniques singularly designed to 'indirectly' rally awareness once you have already fallen asleep and begun to have ordinary dreams. One thereby learns to recognise cues in dreaming that remind you to wake up and become conscious in them. Thus with 'dream-induced' lucid dreaming there really is no control as such nor technique involved besides that of the persistent effort of trying to make it happen and then hoping for the best. A purely 'chuck it and chance it' method! DILDs is an entirely random method requiring a prolonged and protracted effort that can often take months, or even years, to perfect. Moreover, even though you will eventually begin to experience lucid dreaming using such an awkward, if not clumsy, method, it will always remain something that's completely outside of your own volitional control, since recognising and responding to cues within a dream is all you can do. The manner in which DILDs work increases the probability of your having more lucid dreams than otherwise, but that's all there is to it. Unfortunately, the process is somewhat long and drawn out, so that most people just don't have the patience to persevere for long enough to ever realise any decent results. You can, however, rest assured that eventually, and providing you don't lose interest, you *will* begin to start having lucid dreams that way. But only very sporadically and tenuously at first and still with absolutely no guarantee whatsoever of ever having any more of them beyond that of it gradually becoming more and more usual to do so. DILDs do work. Eventually! But only with a process that can rather annoyingly take almost forever to master.

On the other hand, with WILDs, the complete opposite is the case. Moreover, with WILDs whether or not you lucid dream is reduced to being purely a matter of learning to become aware of the different stages of falling asleep and then exploiting them to one's own best advantage. The whole emphasis of the WILD technique depends entirely upon being able to gauge exactly when you have reached the required amount of physical, emotional and mental relaxation and then, when you judge the time is right; consciously and quite deliberately, stepping out into a completely lucid dream reality that to all extents and purposes appears as real as anything can be, all the while knowing that it's only a dream.

The very real and genuine problem with DILDs is that you simply cannot ever know in advance if you are actually going to lucid dream or not, whereas with WILDs you either lucid dream or not by choice alone. The advantage therefore WILDs has over DILDs is pretty obvious. I mean, why gamble on lucid dreaming with DILDS when you can instead bet on a sure thing every time with WILDs? Good question, eh?

The differences between these two widely differing methods are really quite remarkable. The place in awareness one arrives at is probably basically the same in both instances, even though how one arrives there is completely different. The end result is still finding oneself in just about the same general area of altered awareness.

I guess what really puzzles me is that, generally speaking, the vast majority of people seeking the experience of lucid dreaming all tend to go by the DILDs route instead of WILDs. I can't understand why, when it's obvious that even one single experience of WILDs is equal to many, many experiences of DILDs! Perhaps, because, for some inexplicable reason, WILDs, although known about and documented, are considered by the dreaming community to be the more difficult method of the two. I would say quite unjustifiably so.

Another distinct problem with DILDing is that of not always ending up in a lucid dream (when you happen to have one that is) in full possession of your waking memory and mental faculties! A state of awareness perhaps better described as being only 'semi-lucid' in that things in the dream happen more randomly and are thus 'dream-driven'. That, although you may have the distinct impression of actually being in a dreaming situation instead of being awake, the thought and idea remains a vague one and the elements of the dream as such are far more compelling. Someone in such a dream may, for example, talk to you or ask you something and you'll become completely involved in replying. You'll get caught-up in the action at hand, as if you were experiencing a real-life situation instead of only a dreaming one. One's objectivity of actually being in a dreaming situation becomes and remains impaired, so to speak, and it becomes just as easy to fall right back into a non-lucid state completely forgetting that you were even awake at all!

Don't get me wrong, these 'semi-lucid' dreams can still be a whole lot of fun. You can find yourself in all sorts of novel situations (as most of our dreams are) and still know for sure that you're dreaming and just kind of go along with whatever happens to be occurring. It's just that one is not completely lucid and fully in control of oneself in them and is, for instance, far more *impulsive*. Something happens in the dream and you just go along with it. Since full access to normal waking memory is impaired or lacking to varying degrees you fail to question it and drift along just like we do in any ordinary dream. One moment you're in a room and the next outside, whereas with WILDs full lucidity and total recall are always available from beginning to end. With WILDs you enter into the dreaming state with exactly the same awareness you lay down to dream with. Things like semi-lucidity do not even generally occur other than under rather unusual and advanced circumstances (something we'll go into a little more in Part 3 of this book; Advanced Lucid Dreaming).

Suffice to say, for now anyway, that the best way to approach lucid dreaming, especially for the beginner, is definitely from the point of view of WILDs rather than DILDs, if only because WILDs are much easier to induce, and maintain, in terms of experiencing full lucidity and recall from beginning to end.

With DILDs you will never quite know how you are doing it. The entire process is clouded, and so the whole experience borders on the mystical whereas, with WILDs (especially the left-sided version of them) the complete opposite is usually the case. Generally speaking, WILDS seem almost factual compared to the fuzzy vagueness of DILDs.

Finally, with DILDs, disorientation (and the overcoming of it) is the norm. In DILDs one struggles to become aware whilst already having a dream, the challenge to do so being enormous to say the least! With WILDs, clarity and full recall always occur as one enters into the dreaming state from the point of view of 'already' being awake.

If you're new to lucid dreaming, I'd recommend not even bothering with DILDs at all, at least in the initial stages, and go directly to WILDs. If, however, you already have been lucky enough to have some experience of lucid dreaming via DILDs, then I'd say you'd better prepare yourself for a sock in the jaw, if not a complete revolution in terms of your lucid dreaming to date, because – oh boy! – you are going to be so very pleasantly surprised at the contrast (and ease) existing between these two methods!

Waking-Induced Lucid Dreams! Think about it – the ability to enter *directly* into a dreaming state from the point of view of *already* being fully awake and conscious. A method that involves no more guessing games about whether or not you will be able to lucid dream tonight. A method that requires nothing more fancy or expensive to put into practice than your usual sleeping attire and something comfortable to lie down on. And that, when mastered and perfected, basically means lucid dreaming *on* demand to virtually anyone who wants to do it. This is precisely what you're going to learn to do right now. Welcome, then, to the wonderful world of 'Waking-Induced' Lucid Dreaming; WILD!

History, Myths and Legends of Lucid Dreaming

People have always been fascinated by dreams if only because strange things occur in them – inconsistent things, bizarre things, sometimes even really amazing things. Moreover, countless millennia of people having all sorts of weird and wonderful dreams, but not really knowing what's happening to them, has, quite naturally, resulted in some spectacular stories, myths and legends and about what our dreams may or may not *mean* to us in our daily waking lives.

Since dreaming is a natural part of the human condition, virtually every culture worldwide, past and present, tends to have some mention of dreaming in their various histories, myths and legends, some more so than others. Everyone dreams and the things people dream about tend to reflect the familiar objects and activities of their lives and the era in which they live. The Romans, for example, in their time and culture no doubt dreamed about typically Roman activities and beliefs. The Vikings did something similar. Thus, dreams quite naturally tend to reflect everyday life in the societies of their particular time, including the understanding we share of them. The Romans, undoubtedly, dreamed of driving around in chariots and carts while we today dream of cars and aeroplanes, proving that little has really changed except, perhaps, the content of those dreams.

Basically then, we dream of that which we already know and are familiar with, added to which, throughout history people have told each other about the dreams they've had and shared them. It was believed that certain dreams revealed significant things, possibly even portents of the future, good as well as bad, depending on the interpretations of village priests or holy men in more ancient cultures. Such interpretations, on occasion, provided some means of resolving people's personal problems and difficulties. Dreams could be strange, dreams could be revealing, portentous or even frightening; no one really understood what they were but it became an accepted part of everyday life because everyone experienced them and because there was nothing anyone could do about it anyway.

Effectively, with few exceptions throughout history, we have always experienced our dreams solely from the point of view of something to which we are being 'subjected', since dreams are apparently something over which we seem to exert little or no control. For example, anyone who can remember having a particularly disturbing nightmare will, I'm sure, attest to their feelings of helplessness during a particularly bad one, not to mention their sheer sense of relief upon reawakening.

In our own predominantly rational Western culture the same, of course, applies, but with the addition of the likes of Sigmund Freud and Carl Jung who, being the holy men and shamans of our times, have brought dreams and dreaming into the perhaps more reputable realm of science and psychiatry for the purposes of psychoanalysis and therapy. Our dreams, seen in this context, may even reveal hidden aspects of the subconscious mind, all of which makes a kind of contextual sense insofar as unconscious dreams might then just relate to unconscious, hidden aspects of the mind (very logical). Moreover, many reputable scientists have claimed that their dreams actually helped them to find novel solutions to trying problems, all of which may well be true to varying degrees. In fact, I'm sure it's true, especially since many reputable people (Albert Einstein included) have readily attested to their dreams having helped them out in some way in finding creative solutions to pressing problems. However, apart from these random quirks of occasionally useful inspiration, this regular, routine, daily aspect of our lives that involves dreaming on a nightly basis has basically been relegated to mere background noise. Dreams are funny, dreams are weird, dreams may even possibly reveal hidden aspects of the subconscious mind under expert psychoanalysis, but because we have no actual volition in them they remain more or less meaningless to us and, as such, are something not really considered as being a bone-fide activity. Some people may have intense or vivid dreams for no known reason and maybe look forward to having more of them, but beyond that, as a species, we've collectively written-off dreams and dreaming as being nothing particularly useful to us. As a result, dreams remain a mere side issue in people's daily lives.

For sure, some people like to believe there's maybe a kind of deeper symbolism to their dreams; that the images they contain can be interpreted as meaningful. For example, dreaming of losing a tooth or of finding a suitcase stuffed with money (apparently quite a common dream, heh) always means something particularly significant, and maybe it even does, who knows? Otherwise, the whole subject of dreams and dreaming has been pushed into the background and right out to the fringe where just about anyone can say anything they like about it and nobody can really say any different.

Since dreams are apparently of no real rational use to anyone other than the psychologist and folklore dream interpreter, this particular topic has effectively fallen into the general area of almost total disinterest. The only exception to this is perhaps the more recent rise of 'lucid dreaming' as a form of entertainment, with this currently being the standard accepted image and understanding of us all having dreams and dreaming. A rather fixed image that's largely going nowhere, but which, I suggest, is radically altered if and when a more voluntary ability to lucid dream is brought into the equation! Something initially explored and popularised, for example, by Stephen LaBerge and the Lucidity Institute, in the USA.

Lucid dreaming, when readily available and perfected, represents nothing less than the fully conscious utilisation of the virtual reality of the dreaming state in order to further extend one's waking activities. This is something that few cultures in recent human history have concerned themselves about with one or two possible exceptions as previously mentioned.

Nevertheless, there have been quite a few cultures in ancient history that took our ability to lucid dream a little differently, if not completely so, many of which have their own interesting tales and stories. There are, in fact, quite a few to choose from but I think my favourite by far, and the most interesting ones, come from the Australian Aborigines and their spectacular 'Dreamtime' creation stories, along with legends and myths verbally handed down from generation to generation for as long as the Aborigines themselves have existed and can remember. And they are really rather fascinating!

These ancient stories, some of which date back at least 40,000 years and probably far longer, tell of two 'God-like' beings from the Dreamtime that ultimately dreamed our whole world into existence one object and one species at a time. This implies that our whole world, fabulous and extensive though it is, is actually nothing more than just another dream that someone (or something) experienced and willed permanently into existence in just about the same way that we are all capable of creating temporary, but similarly convincing realities, in our ordinary dreams every night. A truly marvellous and unique idea!

The Aborigines themselves are living an unbroken culture of millennia where, apparently, lucid dreaming is more or less taken for granted as a commonplace, daily activity that just about everyone in the community partakes in, old and young alike! This ancient culture is, unfortunately, rapidly disappearing due to the industrialised conversion and destruction of what was once traditional, tribal, Aboriginal land, along with the Aborigines themselves and, of course, most of their sacred ancient dreaming traditions, sites, stories and customs.

For example, and really rather amazingly, Aborigines also believe in the ability to interact in the Dreamtime just as if they were awake, something which undoubtedly gave rise to a more magical kind of culture and belief system in which interactions between the Dreamtime and waking life 'overlapped'. As a result, this became an accepted daily practice, even to the point of involving local dreaming experts in the settling of disputes over nefarious dream activities, crimes apparently committed in dreams, in just about the same way as we would involve the police and a forensic scientist today if someone had committing a horrible crime in the waking world. This is a fascinating idea and a very appealing concept in that people could actually interact with each other, for real, via the vehicle of a lucid dream! I mean, wow, I'd really love to be able to do that, wouldn't you? Meet up with friends and lovers in the virtual reality of a dream and genuinely interact with them? A truly amazing concept! If true!

The point here being that, apart from the shamans' 'mystical business' (whatever that is), this whole area of lucid dreaming still remains relatively unexplored and unmapped by modern standards, so who knows what lucid dreaming could include or maybe entail. All we have so far on the subject, beyond that of modern psychiatry, being vague rumours, myths and folklore that has been handed down to us from ancient cultures. (Future dream pioneers, adventurers and explorers *are* currently being actively sought, however. Heh! So read on.)

There are other notable cultures that had something more to do with their dreaming and dream activities and I could probably pad out this chapter with many more equally fascinating examples, some of which are enough to make one's hair stand on end!

But I think I've already made the point fairly clearly with the Australian Aborigines, whose lucid Dreamtime overlaps into their daily waking world and vice-versa, and as such creates an extension to their day instead of having to endure several hours every night in some kind of 'downtime' just as we all appear to have to do in the west.

Think about it. Just what would it be like to be able to revisit the same dream scene as often as you want and maybe even have some kind of history there, even though time as we know it doesn't work quite the same way in dreaming as it does in the waking world. Effectively, time is much more fluid in dreams and can be fast or slow from your own perspective, depending on many different contributing factors.

Fast or slow, all I know for myself is that there simply never seems to be enough time before I have to cease my lucid dreaming activities and wake up and go live life during the day for a while. Moreover, since being able to 'lucid dream on demand' has changed my life, along with adding a whole new and very exciting chapter to it, so much so that I can hardly wait to get back to it each day!

PART 2 – PRACTICE

Hypnagogia: The Key to WILDs

Most people today, even those who have already experienced it, will tell you that it's quite difficult to learn to lucid dream, and not because it's particularly difficult to do once one is actually doing it – that's the easy part! But rather, with current methods, it's the sheer difficulty initially involved in realising that what one is experiencing is, in fact, a dream! A 'waking up' of oneself in a dream whilst one is *already* asleep and dreaming. This in itself constitutes quite a formidable barrier to have to overcome before the joys of exploring a dreaming state open up and it becomes a working reality. This rather hit and miss affair can go on for months before anything happens, if it *ever* happens.

This being the case, it is little wonder then that lucid dreaming is still a rarity, if not a completely unheard of activity, for the majority of people. Moreover, of those who *have* heard of it, many just can't be bothered to make the prolonged effort required to give themselves the chance to experience something as nebulous as *maybe* having a lucid dream. And who can really blame them? Lucid dreaming is a fascinating concept and, if you understand it, a very attractive one. However, the fact that there are no clear steps to accomplish it other than waiting around for it to occur, often for months on end, is, quite understandably, off-putting to most people. Thankfully, there is a better way.

The key to lucid dreaming is 'hypnagogia' and lies in the realisation of how sleep itself occurs, functions and works, given that there are only two basic ways of falling asleep. One can either be induced into a somnolent state in the normal way and, as a result, automatically experience average unconscious random dreams, or one can both *deliberately* and *quite consciously* enter into it, in which case one automatically experiences lucid dreams.

The choice is ours, although in most cases no conscious choice is ever made beyond that of getting into bed, lying there and waiting for sleep to descend. This being the 'unconscious' method; a method that has become completely ingrained in us throughout the course of our lives! This is effectively a default method insofar as no one ever consciously *tries* to go to sleep, sleep being something that just happens as far as most people are concerned. Getting tired, feeling drowsy, laying down and letting sleep overtake us, is a pattern that people have learned to recognise. This is something we've all learned to let happen and no one questions it. It seems so natural! After all, it's what we've done ever since we were babies. We get tired and need to sleep, and that's all there is to it! Right?

Wrong! That's not all there is to it; only in terms of mundane practicality is that the case, and accordingly, that that's all people have cared to know about it. Get tired enough and you fall asleep; who needs to know more?

The truth is, people don't really *want* to sleep, they *have* to, since sleep is such a seemingly normal and accepted daily activity, to the point that we even have rooms in our homes set aside for the express purposes of doing so; bedrooms! The fact is that we all spend around a third of our lives sleeping. Live sixty years and you'll likely have spent twenty of them sawing logs (snoring Zzzzz) which, if you think about it, is such a waste of time. Love it or hate it, we all have to do it.

Most people don't pay any attention to it, but on the way into sleep, if you are watching, you will likely become aware of slight colours and faint images that seem to appear at random before you as you lie there in the dark with your eyes closed. Streaks of shifting colours, speckled coloured dots like newsprint, morphing geometric shapes; all these fleeting patterns and images are called *hypnagogia.*

Most people can, for example, probably remember having had a fairly vivid experience of hypnagogia at some point in their lives, if only because, on occasion, they've had a couple of drinks too many at a party and can remember a bunch of lights and swirling images dancing before their eyes (smiling from experience) just before they conked out on some stranger's rather damp and probably smelly bathroom floor. (Heh, I still have the t-shirt for that! But don't wear it anymore.)

Anyway, I'm not going to go into a long, technical description of this visual phenomenon as such, detailed information being readily available online for anyone to find (a remarkable 152,000 pages currently according to Google). Hypnagogia can take many forms, ranging all the way from just some very slight blobs and shifting streaks of colour – through reasonably clear scenes and images – to full-blown, startlingly vivid and seemingly frozen or moving images of just about every shape, vista and possible description. These effects appear to everyone on their way into sleep as they are lying there maybe mulling over a bunch of thoughts, many of which consist of pictures as well as words and sometimes even sounds. So we lie there letting all this happen while not really paying much attention to it, and then, the next thing you know, you're whisked off into sleep and dreams without ever remembering the exact moment of doing so. This, as it turns out, just so happens to be the perfect recipe for falling asleep on a dime (an American euphemism for falling asleep in an instant), something all you insomniacs out there may want to pay attention to and use as a potentially useful, express method of inducing sleep in only a few moments. A cure for insomnia as such when deliberately applied.

We usually go into sleeping mode in a totally unconscious, non-deliberate manner by letting whatever it is that *makes* us sleep pull us involuntarily into it merely by hanging around in that dreamy/sleepy zone for a long enough period of time. This, of course, is something we all had to learn to do. Children, for example, often exhibit difficulty in falling asleep even though they are completely worn out. This is mainly because they are still in the process of learning this default method of going to sleep, as opposed to something they can deliberately choose to turn on and turn off at will.

Try a little experiment yourself tonight when you lay down to sleep. Don't attempt anything unusual as such, try simply to observe the sleep process as it naturally unfolds for you. Chances are your observations will be cut short as you're suddenly pulled into an unconscious state, but make the attempt anyway, if only to start consciously familiarising yourself with what is normally a wholly unconscious process.

Entering into sleep in such an unconscious manner automatically results in ordinary, random, non-lucid dreams, something which seems quite obvious, if you think about it. Whereas to enter into the sleeping state consciously and deliberately instead, results in something else altogether. It results in dreams again, but this time fully lucid ones in which one is completely aware of being in a dreaming state and can control their dreams to varying degrees depending on what you want (and know) to do with them. Furthermore, the only real difficulty people might experience in attempting to lucid dream is basically that of correcting and getting over our more usual, sloppy habit of just letting ourselves be pulled into sleep in a completely unconscious manner.

If I appear to be belabouring this point, it is because I believe that this particular realisation rests at the very crux of understanding exactly what ordinary dreams and lucid dreams are and why they occur. Namely, that what we usually call 'falling asleep' is, in fact, the *unconscious* entering into an available altered state of awareness, one that somehow energetically refreshes the body and mind and one to which we return night after night but only because we have to. This is due to the notion that maintaining consciousness for sixteen hours is somehow costly in terms of energy; energy that needs to be replenished with both food and sleep.

As previously mentioned, as very young babies, we cannot be awake and grow at the same time due to our small physical size and lack of stored energy. We do, however, gradually accumulate enough strength through food and sleep to remain awake for longer and longer periods of time between feeds until eventually, as adults, we can just about sustain sixteen hours of being awake in every twenty-four.

The point is, that *if* we have to enter into sleep whether we like it or not every sixteen hours or so, then there's no reason why we should enter into that sleep in a totally unconscious manner if we don't have to. This is precisely what lucid dreaming is! This also explains and highlights the sheer difficulty of DILDs in that one is already almost completely unconscious even before trying to activate them.

The fact is, with DILDs, one relies on realising that one is already in a dream and dreaming. A phenomenal achievement as far as I'm concerned and to which I respectfully tip my hat to anyone who's ever managed it. In my humble opinion, this just goes to show what people can do when they really put their minds to something: we can apparently achieve even the impossible.

Given the choice, I can't possibly see the attraction of using such a difficult method, especially when there's a much more sensible and straightforward approach available. I mean, why go to sleep and *hope* to wake up later in a dream when you can just go straight into a lucid dreaming situation from the point of view of still being wide awake? Could it be that we just don't realise that we can?

As far as I can tell, the only *real* difficulty with lucid dreaming is finding and getting one's 'sea-legs,' so to speak. Upon entering into lucid dreaming, one is forced to strike a kind of emotional balance between remaining in the dream or waking up from it. Nothing can do that for you except the accumulated experience of having done it many times. The only way to lucid dream is by lucid dreaming! As with everything, the more you do the better you get; it's as simple as that.

All one *really* has to do in order to *start* lucid dreaming, is to learn to recognise the stages of falling asleep, find this hypnagogia on the way into it and then treat these hypnagogic images in a very particular way. Ultimately, it is through hypnagogia that one actually enters into an altered state at all and lucid dreaming in particular. Should you at any time opt to dream normally again, then, by all means, just lay back and watch the shifting movie show images and before you know it you'll be fast asleep in no time. On the other hand, when you want to lucid dream, then all you do is to watch that same movie show again, only this time treating those hypnagogic images by examining their detail in a particular way.

This conscious act of examining a hypnagogic image's finer detail is the very thing that finally beckons one right into a lucid dream. One is somehow bodily zoomed in, or rather, pulled into the image itself resulting in dreams in which one is already awake. Not examining the details of those images while just letting yourself drift as usual results in one eventually nodding-off and having very ordinary, non-lucid dreams...and really that's all there is to it. A simple choice!

Newbies to lucid dreaming often find this sudden, drastic change of perspective to be a little shocking to say the least, and will immediately start talking to themselves in a very excited manner about how they've finally done it –wow! They don't realise that this kind of excitable behaviour, both mental and emotional, is virtually guaranteed to quickly end the whole experience prematurely (at which point they will hear Homer Simpson's voice again). This 'D'oh! factor' (heh) is a common feature that's basically unavoidable for all newbies until they learn in dreaming to turn on their heel with impunity and to go off exploring, instead of standing around congratulating themselves on having arrived. This is something that everyone goes through at the beginning. Persist, however, and in the end your ability to enter quite consciously into a dreaming state and then maintain it for longer and longer periods of time will bloom, eventually opening up a whole new world to be explored and enjoyed entirely at your own leisure. Hypnagogia is the key that genuinely opens that door.

Relaxation Techniques

There are many ways of achieving a state of relaxation. You may already know some and be using them fairly regularly anyway. If so, that's just fine as it will definitely save you time later while becoming familiar with using a state of relaxation as a springboard into lucid dreaming.

Okay, so this is where the fun really begins. Better sit down and strap in, since for our current purposes I'll be concentrating on just one or two quite simple but effective methods of getting oneself sufficiently relaxed to invoke our hidden, innate ability to hop off into a waking dream state at will. Both methods are rather similar.

For the first I'd initially suggest getting yourself into bed and lying down on your left side with your knees together and your legs slightly bent. Give your body a little time to adjust to the exertion involved of getting into bed and settling down into a comfortable position. Just lie there for a few minutes in the dark until your breathing and heart-rate gradually slow down to a steady rhythm.

After about five minutes, when your breathing has settled right down and has become steady and regular, deliberately take a long, deep breath by breathing slowly in through your nose until no more air can get in. Don't force anything or cork your throat by letting go and relaxing your chest once fully inflated. Keep your throat held open and hold that breath for about four or five seconds or so and then let it out again very slowly through the mouth while at the same time trying to feel any residual tension in your muscles draining out of your body and sinking down through the bed and into the floor. Make a conscious attempt *as* you breathe out to feel your whole body becoming even more relaxed than it was before, as though it was sinking down into the bed. Aim via these breaths to let your body become so relaxed that if anyone were at one point to lift one of your arms and let it go again, the arm would just flop right back to where it was under its own weight without any help from you. Do this long breath just the once and then let your body return to breathing again under its own steam. Spend a few moments breathing normally, just letting your body breathe as it may, and then, after a little while, deliberately take another long slow breath in through your nose feeling your whole body tense up slightly as you control the intake of air, letting your lungs fill up as much as they can without forcing anything, again holding that breath when it reaches the top by maintaining the ever so slight pressure of breathing in (i.e. by not corking your throat in order to hold it locked in) for another count of four or five seconds before slowly letting that breath out through your mouth while at the same time deliberately letting go of your body as though you were weightless. When all the air is naturally out (again without forcing anything) let your body return to its usual way of breathing for a couple of minutes or so, noting how much more your body feels relaxed each time.

Repeat this exercise several times over the course of the next few minutes and you'll probably be surprised at just how tense you actually were, even though your body felt completely relaxed before. A good example of this is around the head, neck and shoulders area which seems to sink ever deeper than before into the pillow each time you do the long breath out. Try to detect any residual muscle tension from your body sink down into the bed and floor as a mild sensation similar to that of going down in an elevator. Pay particular attention to these areas of the head, neck and shoulders, working through them in sequence if necessary until they all feel completely relaxed and as sunken into your pillow as they're likely to get.

Keep this up for about ten to twenty minutes in total, alternating between normal breathing and the occasional long controlled one and/or until you experience a sensation of feeling like a complete dead weight, trying each time to aim for that feeling of being so relaxed that if someone were to lift your arm and let it go again it would just flop back to your side.

You may also feel at this point a very slight overall tingling sensation, a kind of spreading numbness in your limbs, and also notice that your breathing is now beginning to be composed of slow, far slighter breaths coming more from the lower part of your abdomen (belly breaths). This is perfect. Don't try to force this situation to come about, let it occur naturally through using your breathing to release muscle tension. This is precisely the easy state of mental and physical relaxation one is aiming for in order to begin trying to lucid dream, and this feeling of bodily lightness or largeness coupled with belly breaths confirms it.

The second method consists of doing exactly the same breathing exercises for a few moments to get started, but this time systematically working all the way up from your toes to the top of your head, gradually releasing all bodily tension from each area down through the bed and into the ground as you go. Again, spending at least fifteen to twenty minutes or so on this, the time it takes to reach a state of relaxation gradually becoming shorter with each session as your ability to relax at will progresses. Don't worry if it takes longer in the initial stages, you are learning to *consciously* relax your body and it takes a little practice. You may have to try for forty minutes the first few times to reach and recognise this state of being but, rest assured, you'll quickly get it all down to under twenty minutes or so with familiarity and practice. In the meantime, just enjoy it for what it is; the setting out upon a new adventure. Don't rush things. Enjoy every part and stage of it!

In order later to reach a state of lucid dreaming, it's also very important during these relaxation exercises not to move or change your body position or posture at all, particularly during the last few minutes of doing them. During the first few minutes get yourself into a comfortable enough position and try to maintain it and to also perfect that position by tweaking it minutely here and there until you don't need to settle down or move anymore. After that don't even move an inch.

The end result of relaxing without moving like this is eventually to achieve a mild sensation of floating, or of the body having slightly expanded in some way. At this point the hands will possibly sometimes feel kind of puffy or enlarged. Other times it's as though one can no longer tell the exact proportion or size of bodily areas you happen to focus on. For example, upon focusing on them my teeth once lost their usual dimensions of size, feeling huge and disproportionate for the size of my mouth until they felt the size of tombstones. A very odd sensation indeed, but I stress that all these minor sensations are perfectly normal, they're a novelty, enjoy them and explore them for what they are, they are nothing to worry about and are really only clues the body provides us with to let us know we're nearly ready now to enter into a lucid dreaming state.

Once you've reached this floating feeling of relaxation, the next step is to absolutely and deliberately turn your attention *completely away* from all and any sensations of the body altogether, totally ignoring them. Having served their purpose they are no longer important. Peer instead at the blank dark screen you can see just behind your closed eyes. Don't move at all and hang on to that feeling of lightness or floating and stare at the darkness that's right there in front of your face until you begin to notice the odd blob or streak of colour appearing and disappearing at random. Your body may feel a little strange at this point but just totally ignore it (or any other sensations) by deliberately placing and holding your full attention 'only' on what your eyes can see.

At this point, consciously adjust your focus so it's as though you are looking at an area about ten to fifteen inches away from your face. Keep your eyes closed and let any blobs and splashes of colour come and go as they please. Don't attempt to control these effects in any way, just keep watching for them by staring straight ahead until you perhaps notice the appearance of an image of some kind. This is the next stage.

The following images can be rather faint and fleeting (fast), not really giving you the time to focus on them properly, but that's okay, don't worry about it, just let them come and go as they please and wait for the next one to appear. Having already made yourself relax you shouldn't be thinking about your body or your breathing at all by having deliberately forced your attention away from them onto only what your closed eyes can see. Don't try to do anything other than watch those images come and go, the same way as those blobs and streaks of colour did, especially since at this point you are nearly ready to attempt entering into a dreaming state.

The only problem you may initially encounter at this stage is that of accidentally drifting right off into a deep sleep, and this is something that's quite likely to happen repeatedly until you learn to recognise this as being a distinct possibility. After all, every night for the duration of our lives to date, we've always piled into bed with the express expectation of getting off to sleep as quickly as possible. We never know, or even remember, just exactly how (or when) we actually drifted off, but usually just lie there kind of relaxing and getting comfortable while waiting to be somehow snatched away.

It's a ritual we've all unconsciously learned to perform since before we were born. One feels kind of drowsy and the eyes close while not really thinking of anything in particular, and before you know it we've gone off to sleep without even realising it. Suddenly it's the next day, something we're all totally expert at doing by now because we've been doing it all our lives. Children (and insomniacs) are the only ones who tend to exhibit any difficulty in getting off to sleep sometimes and so we distract them by reading them stories and singing them lullabies and as soon as they stop struggling against it their little eyes glaze over and off they jolly well go! (Peace reigns at last. Whew!)

But I digress...so anyway, keep going like this, lightly gazing at fleeting images while trying not to accidentally nod off completely, until a really clear image shows up, sometimes shockingly so! Next, do your best to let your eyes examine some of that image's details.

This image could be of anything; a tree, a partial view of a scene of some sort, someone's faint face in profile, whatever. It doesn't really matter what the image is, just attempt to keep that image within view by deliberately examining its details. Don't fixate your eyes on any single aspect of that image or attempt to try to force anything because the likelihood is that it'll just vanish away only to be replaced with another moments later. If not, just go back to watching the dark space and blobs of colour that are roughly about fifteen or so inches from your face from behind your closed eyes until another image appears all by itself.

You may experience several sessions like this (vague images and sometimes clearer ones) and then inadvertently drift off to sleep before anything else can happen. This is all quite normal so keep this practice up. Everyone has spent a lifetime unconsciously relaxing and going straight off to sleep, a habit you are now trying to break by becoming conscious of the process itself. Moreover, at one point along this road you'll encounter a startlingly clear image that appears frozen, so clear that you'll experience an irresistible need to open your eyes just to make sure that they're still actually closed.

Again, this may happen to you several times before you get to the point that you can eventually resist the temptation to throw open your eyes each time just to check. Something which is surprisingly difficult to resist as it appears to be some kind of an unconscious reflex that takes time to learn to overcome. Relax and let things go at their own pace. Your only real job at this point is to observe these images and not let yourself fall fast asleep as per usual.

Anyway, keep trying and you *will* eventually succeed in absorbing the mild jolt involved in being confronted with these startlingly clear images and being able to maintain your focus on only the images themselves instead of yourself and how you feel (which, you're supposed to be deliberately ignoring and looking away from anyway – remember?).

Again, the only drawback at this point is that of maybe falling fast asleep in an instant only to wake up what seems like only moments later, albeit in truth hours have passed, wondering what the hell happened plus where has the night gone. Then again, not to worry – ha! ha! It's an expected effect, so just try to laugh it off. Don't get annoyed, for example, at yourself through being perplexed by strange events. This is all part of the learning curve. Just try again, and again, and even again – I think you probably get the picture. Eventually, something changes and you stop falling asleep or opening your eyes each time, whereupon a series of seemingly even more really clear images show up. These images are so vivid, in fact, that you're suddenly right back to automatically popping open your eyes just to make sure they're still actually closed. This may reoccur several times before you finally manage to resist the reflex urge involved. However, just like the last time and after a few experiences of it, you'll quickly learn to compensate. This is another very good lesson and practice for you because what comes next is even more startling; images so clear and sharp that they are a wonder to behold! Having got over snapping open your eyes every time, you can now begin to examine these incredibly clear images with more ease. It's just like being at the movies and just watching them is a minor wonder in itself.

At this point you now have two choices. The first of which is to carry on watching and wondering (plus enjoying) this really incredible experience just for its own sake, in which case at some point you'll likely fall fully fast asleep and wake up the next day as usual. Watching these really clear images for any length of time (a marvellous experience though it is) always leads to falling away into normal sleep. On the other hand, if you instead stare at one of them and attempt to examine the finer details of it, something very strange happens; a sensation of what can only really be described as a kind of 'zooming-in' – and then you'll suddenly find yourself in a fully lucid dreaming state.

Well done, you've just made it into your very first waking-induced lucid dream! You've just gone WILD. (Yeeea!)

However, will you be able to maintain it or will you be immediately booted straight back out for bad behaviour? By this I mean that the almost incredible jolt one experiences in this initial stage of 'entering' is almost too much to handle because, just as your eyes kept popping open seemingly all by themselves at an earlier stage, the physical and mental jolt of realisation that this sudden movement produces can at first be overwhelming. For example, when I first got to this stage, many a time I'd inadvertently, without any seeming volition whatsoever, literally sit bolt upright in bed with my eyes wide open before even knowing or realising what was going on – yikes! This is the only way to describe it. Added to which, you can't seem to do anything about it except laugh on each occasion because it's so unexpected. (It really is quite shocking, heh! heh!) Yikes! Followed immediately by "What the…?" (I'm still laughing – because it's such a funny and unexpected reaction each time, even when you're prepared for it). Furthermore, this reaction is something that takes time and patience to 'get over', as was the case with the eyes popping open thingy too. It's another reflex action that even being mentally prepared for doesn't tame. The only thing that succeeds in overcoming it is experiencing it enough times until some 'inner' (rather than intellectual) adjustment gets made and you eventually stop reacting quite so violently to the transition. It is at this point that the whole field of lucid dreaming suddenly opens up to you.

So, could entering into lucid dreaming really be as simple as this; so *uncomplicated*? Is it really just a matter of relaxing in the correct manner and sequence and off you go fully awake from the get-go…every time? And I mean *every* time!

Well folks, this *is* the secret of doing it. (If you can call it a secret exactly because it's so simple it's a joke!) This is it, in its entirety! That's *all* there is to it, and, as such, you can do it whenever you like. Lucid dreaming 'on demand' every time you so wish. Although, for the life of me, I can't see any reason why anyone would ever want to return to normal sleep and dreams after this – can you?

As soon as one overcomes the unconscious urge to sit bolt upright at the point of transition, the dream doors are then thrown wide open and the world of lucid dreaming becomes your proverbial oyster and playground. And that, my friends is the technique, all of it. The whole *Cannoli*!

The rest of this book is quite simply about how to perfect this technique so that 'lucid dreaming on demand' becomes a daily reality.

Enjoy!

Entering the Lucid Dreaming State

Entering into lucid dreaming follows the same process as entering into ordinary random dreaming, the only difference being that via WILDs one enters into that dreaming state consciously and deliberately instead of unconsciously and accidentally. Fall asleep, as per normal, and at some point you'll have normal, random dreams, something that genuinely makes the DILD version of lucid dreaming so difficult to put into practice. Enter into the dream state consciously however, as is the case with WILDs, and that dreaming state is experienced in a completely different way; as lucid dreams with full waking awareness right from the start, and with the added bonus of experiencing no interruption to one's stream of waking awareness.

It takes a little practice to prolong the experience upon having arrived in a lucid dreaming state. A slight mistake here or an emotional wobble there and, wallop, you're automatically and involuntarily 'booted out' of lucid dreaming back to the looking at hypnagogia stage. This abrupt change of perspective is often accompanied by a fairly startling 'zinging' sensation (Zing!) which is, of course, immediately followed by 'D'oh!' upon realising that you've again dropped the ball. This is something that, somewhat frustratingly, happens time and again until you eventually learn to strike a very particular and peculiar mental and emotional balance which we'll look into and discuss right now.

So, okay, you've learned and practiced the simple enough relaxation exercises. More importantly, you've learned not to move around at all while doing them until you begin consciously to enter into the first stages of sleep.

You've consciously and deliberately paused there for a while and played around with hypnagogia until the first in a series of particularly sharp images begins to appear, so sharp and clear that many times you've been forced to open your eyes in surprise just in order to check that they are still actually closed (D'oh!). You've then learned to resist that imperative urge to open them and to keep your eyes closed regardless of whether they are open or not until, fairly soon, increasingly vivid images start to appear. Well done, because now you're ready to go on to the next stage.

By now you should be seeing hypnagogic image after image in fairly rapid succession. Wait then until a particularly clear one shows up and attempt to 'arrest' it. I've no idea why this occurs but apparently deliberately examining the details of any one image – the clearer and sharper it is to begin with, the better – has the distinct effect of making it remain in view for longer. Just keep doing this even if the image fades or changes into another one. That's okay, just let it happen.

The main thing, at this point, is to be consciously selecting from among the clearest and most vivid hypnagogic images that appear the one you're going to attempt to 'arrest'. This is the practice, because somewhere along the line of attempting to do this 'arresting of images' something rather amazing and miraculous happens. At one moment you'll be gazing at some image and probably marvelling at just how clear and vivid it really is this time, when, without any warning whatsoever, there's that 'zing' feeling again, only *this* time it all goes the other way and you're literally pulled right *into* a fully-fledged dreaming scenario. This is usually followed immediately by: Yikes! Zing! D'oh! in that order (laughing) as you bounce right back out of it again to exactly where you were only just a moment ago (double D'oh!).

Okay, let's keep things light-hearted...let's have another go...stare at that next incredibly clear image that's just turned up, begin deliberately examining its finer details in order to arrest it... and before you know it, zing! You're powerfully pulled right back into another (or even the same) dreaming scene. You look around a bit. You realise yet again that you're actually lucid dreaming. You try your best this time not to overreact in any way but it's just so exciting! It's really happening. Zing! D'oh! So, okay, let's have another go. Zing! You're back in. Zing! You're straight back out again. D'oh! (Really laughing at the memory of doing this myself so many times, hahaha!)

Each time it happens, however, it's as though you're learning a little more, then a little more, and then a little more and so on, until the moment arrives that you're in a lucid dream long enough to attempt doing something other than flitting back and forth between lying down awake and dreaming. Now, *this* is the opportunity to have your first full and proper lucid dream 'for real', something which is achieved, once started, by literally turning on one's heel both mentally and emotionally, so to speak, and instead of pondering upon what's happening to you and how marvellous it all is, you just turn on your heel and go off...exploring!

You slowed those images down and kept them in view by deliberately examining their details. And then you even allowed yourself to be pulled right into one of them, and now, here you are, standing in a fully-fledged lucid dream, only you really don't know what to do with yourself next or how to control it. This is so cool.

The point is that, after all your hard work, (which wasn't really so hard after all, was it?) right here at this juncture and/or point of departure is where the *real* journey and practice of lucid dream discovery begins. Furthermore, you can also rest assured that from now on the transition between waking and lucid dreaming will only improve and get faster the more you do it until eventually, with very little practice and within only a few minutes of lying down, you'll be straight off into a lucid dream with almost no bother at all. This, incidentally, is precisely the way it should be done if your dream state is to be genuinely enjoyed, explored and mapped.

Oddly enough, the first few times you genuinely enter into lucid dreaming may seem like protracted experiences with several distinct stages. Try to make mental notes of these without particularly emphasising them because, later, you may find that the particular way you got into, and experienced, lucid dreaming those first few times, can be quite revealing about your own inner nature and predilection. Moreover, later you will probably stop noticing these things altogether as the transition into lucid dreaming increasingly becomes something that happens almost instantaneously.

In other words, eventually, you'll quickly get to the place in relaxation where dreaming occurs and see an image, examine its details and then step right into it, no fuss, no bother. Stepping back out again is exactly the same, thus you can be either 'in' a lucid dream or not at will. This is something I've termed 'lucid dreaming on demand'. In fact, flitting back and forth a few times between dreaming and waking like that seemingly has the effect of clearing out all the cobwebs. Then you'll know *exactly* not only what lucid dreaming actually is but also how to do it, and perhaps, even more importantly, *why* you are now able to do it.

At this point in the learning curve lucid dreaming becomes merely a choice one makes (to dream or not to dream, that is the question?) and after getting into the right state of relaxation you can step off into a dream which you can see right there waiting for you. Alternatively, of course, you can lean the other way that leads back to lying down awake in bed, or, rather interestingly, you can even hold back at a kind of 'midway-point' that is neither awake nor dreaming and from which point of view you can now see both options as existing equally.

This 'middle ground' is something I initially overlooked in favour of immediately leaping into lucid dreams just about as fast as I could. (I'd been trying for so long that I didn't want to mess about and, at first, I grabbed each and every opportunity to lucid dream, believe me!)

Anyway, be that as it may, I do think that reaching this midway point and acknowledging its existence is an important development that needs to be investigated further, and we'll definitely come back to this subject later on. The main thing for now is that you've now begun, at last, to be able to get into a lucid dream almost, but not quite yet, on demand. Rest assured, however, the more you accomplish lucid dreaming the more it happens, almost as if with practice an inner barrier within ourselves suddenly falls under the impact of actually having these experiences.

The challenges involved, apparently, are not those of learning a new or difficult technique so much as gradually learning to overcome *already* learned and established reactionary behaviours in ourselves, both mental and emotional. In dreams the world appears as it always has and does; there is ground and sky along with all the familiar objects of the daily world which, to all intents and purposes, are almost exactly the same as in the waking world. The only real difference between them being the way one has to relearn to conduct oneself in either state. One's emotional and mental reaction to things has to be slightly modified in those dream worlds, almost as if they demand a kind of emotional and mental detachment from them. However, one thing's for sure; behave and react as you'd normally do in the waking world and that's precisely where you'll very quickly find yourself every time. This becomes most noticeable upon awakening where the mood of lucid dreaming is often carried over into the waking world, sometimes for hours afterwards. This experience is not dissimilar to that of having been away from home for a couple of weeks and noticing how things all seem to look a little different somehow upon returning. For example, streets appear somehow smaller or narrower, the area seems a little more quaint than you perhaps remember it, rooms in your apartment appear smaller or larger than you remember them, perhaps also a little grubbier and maybe in need of airing. Things are exactly how and where you remember them, yet somehow all slightly different, almost as if you're not quite altogether there yet. Something is lacking, a feeling of familiarity, possibly. This sensation persists for sometimes another two or three days but also noticeably gradually wears off until eventually everything appears and feels as it always did. You're back!

The same applies to the sensation of re-entering the waking world after having lucid dreamed, since for a little while one is noticeably not quite yet oneself, feeling clearly energised from the experience and yet somewhat detached. A kind of 'inner silence' prevails. In fact, this is the self-same mood that allowed one to maintain a lucid dream and look around in it without getting booted straight back out into waking. It's a lingering mood that, for a little while at least, may well provide the opportunity of examining the waking world from the same perspective, perceiving it almost as if one were still in a lucid dream or had just returned home after being away.

Whatever mood you happen to have been in previously, always takes a moment to change over to the other mood and vice versa. Upon entering into dreaming one has to struggle to somewhat suspend one's otherwise normal analytical and emotional responses to things, while the reverse is also true in that upon returning to the waking world one equally struggles to turn those same features back on. In any case, everyone already experiences this every single time they wake up, albeit unconsciously, and is something which we more usually refer to as not yet being 'fully awake'. This is so commonplace to us that we take it completely for granted as part of the sleeping process. The reversal of this also occurs every time we tire and need to go to sleep, in that we're swept along with a feeling of pleasing lethargy and fatigue. We yawn and stretch and our eyes feel heavy. It becomes hard to remain focused on ideas. Dialogue on the TV for instance becomes background noise and then we know it's time for bed. The fact of the matter is that we already know all there is to know about this whole process of falling asleep and waking up again. Having done so all our lives, it's become completely second nature to us. Moreover, we unquestioningly accept the symptoms and effects going in both directions as being normal, particularly those of falling asleep and having ordinary, chaotic, commonplace dreams. Enter into dreaming consciously from the point of view of already being awake, however, and it all becomes a completely different ball game. Oh yes! It certainly does! 'Being awake' changes everything!

This 'realisation of process' might just provide some answers to age old questions, such as, what is sleep and why do we dream? Or rather, why do we all have to fall asleep and have weird disassociated dreams anyway? In which case the answer now seems fairly obvious; that falling asleep in an unconscious manner *automatically* gives rise to ordinary random type dreams, dreams in which we're ostensibly fast asleep. On the other hand, entering *consciously* into dreaming has the complete opposite effect. One has dreams in which one is completely awake. Lucid dreams! The reason people have ordinary dreams is simply because they always enter into them in an unconscious manner.

The same also applies when maintaining the dreaming state. In the same way you deliberately focused your attention on the hypnagogia instead of one's bodily sensations, this is exactly what one now has to do to keep the lucid dream going and not getting booted out. Attention is deliberately pulled away from the 'self' and focused instead on the specific details of the dream. It couldn't be more simple, or more consistent, than what you've already been doing all along. Effectively, one is deliberately quelling the rational mind in favour of observing and examining the details of whatever one is confronted with instead of focusing on what one might normally think or feel about it. Thus one learns to *accept* things rather than judging them and being forced to react accordingly, depending on what one has already learned to do. It's really as simple as that! What is not simple, however, is to adapt these otherwise already ingrained reactions and responses to ordinary situations and things, which is why, in the initial stages at least, and paradoxically so, we regularly get booted out; not in spite of, but rather, because of them.

Levels of Lucidity

To call them 'levels' as such might not be entirely accurate because, instead of different levels stacked vertically, this is likely to be merely the result of a subjective impression, rather than the reality, and could just as easily be something more horizontally linear. For the purpose of talking about it, however, I've opted to go with the vertical approach and to speak in terms of depth to describe what appears to be, if not levels exactly, then some kind of stacked layers that give a distinct impression of depth. Either way, it's not really that important *how* it's described and you will no doubt come around to formulating your own ideas when you encounter it in the course of your own dreaming, as you no doubt will, but which will suffice here for reason of discussion.

So what do I mean by 'depth' exactly, and where does all this come into dreams and lucid dreaming in particular? Well, in the types of lucid dreams generated by the DILD method, levels of depth do not really seem to come into the picture much, if at all. Dream-induced dreams nearly always plunge the dreamer, by default, into a fairly deep level of dreaming right from the outset. Presumably, this is because the person is fast asleep and already having a dream involving many complicated factors and potential distractions with which whatever remains of their conscious mind is already fully preoccupied. Suddenly becoming lucid at that precise moment also means taking-on and handling all the particular complications of that specific dream in which they suddenly wake up in and find themselves. The struggle to do so under such circumstances, coupled with that of also trying to maintain a reasonable degree of lucidity in them, can be very challenging, to say the least. And perhaps, in part, accounts for why it usually takes so very long to start to gain any headway using the dream-induced method. Being plunged right into the deep end, as one ordinarily is via DILDs, is doubly disorientating and taxes one's lucidity to the utmost as the struggle is always, at least initially, one of just being able to maintain that lucidity, no matter how fragile, leaving little time or attention to notice anything else like subtleties of degree.

Fortunately, with WILDs, the opposite is again always the case, in that one quite naturally starts off at the topmost level or layer, the easiest of all in which to be lucid, and, more importantly, the easiest to maintain one's lucidity in. Next, with experience, successively working your way down through the other various levels existing underneath as your experience and familiarity with handing yourself in the dream state increases. Just how far or how many of these 'levels' extend underneath is currently unknown and thus remains unmapped. However, experience tends to suggest that there are several distinct levels, four of which I'm currently aware of and which I'll shortly attempt to describe, but I suspect that there are probably a lot more, that other more talented dreamers than myself can discover and eventually map. Not only for themselves, but also for the growing community of lucid dreamers out there who are also interested in mapping and exploring these altered states of consciousness.

The very first level you'll encounter via a WILD will always reassuringly be what I've temporarily called the 'training program' or 'construct' of *The Matrix* movie fame. This is something other explorers will undoubtedly later rename perhaps more accurately. In this instance, in a lucid dream, the only person in that dream will be you and you alone. Initial images of being in either a room or an outside setting do not really figure so much with these starter dreams; what really counts in this 'training area' is the highly coveted level of ultra-clear, full lucidity, complete with full access to all your normal waking memories and thoughts. This is a decidedly rare occurrence with DILDs, especially in the initial stages. Of course, full lucidity and full memory are crucial to intelligently deciding just exactly what you're going to be doing next with all of this. A clarity that is often singularly lacking in the shifting, semi-lucid levels of awareness that, more often than not, typically go hand in hand with DILDs. Enter into lucid dreaming via a DILD and you'll be straightway nearly overwhelmed and struggle to find your feet. Enter into lucid dreaming via a WILD, however, and you'll be automatically fully aware of what's going on right from the outset. Not only will you be fully aware of what's happening to you, but you will also remember exactly who you are and what you are and what you have been attempting to do right up till that very moment. You'll have full awareness and full waking memory to assist you. Effectively, therefore this is the area (or first level) in which you may not only familiarise yourself with the conditions of being in a dreaming state, but also be able to experiment to some degree with manipulating yourself whilst in such an altered state of awareness. For example, the 'training program' is the perfect environment for the beginner in lucid dreaming to practice their flying abilities (very cool). The thing to do initially is to return to this training area as regularly as possible in order to become proficient in getting used to handling yourself in the dreaming state before moving onto applying these skills in perhaps more distant and/or busier levels.

The next level down is similar to the first, except that there may well be one or two other people moving around in there doing their own thing, but with whom you probably won't have any direct interaction. Initially, this level is more difficult to remain fully lucid in. Consider, for example, that you move from the first level to the second, there will be a noticeably longer moment in which you struggle to remain fully lucid; though still lucid enough to know that you're dreaming. The full lucidity you've already become accustomed to expecting on the first level noticeably struggles to come to the fore for a few moments, unlike the first level wherein full lucidity is always automatic. However, after a short while it clears up again and you are once again fully lucid. It may seem to take extra effort to maintain this level but you soon get used to it and then carry on as before; exploring. You wobble around a bit initially, noticing the extra difficulty involved for a few moments and then everything clears up all by itself. It's not like you actually have to do anything other than maintain it until your lucidity stabilises all by itself. Basically, all you have to do is linger there long enough until some unconscious internal adjustment is made and then you carry on as normal.

It is yet more difficult to remain lucid in the third level than in the previous two. Lucidity at this level drifts away from you and returns like waves. You still know that you're dreaming but the drop in full lucidity is quite noticeable. You struggle to arrange your thoughts and for a while it's like mentally wading through water. It's difficult to think or even remember what you were trying to do, but don't be surprised if, at this point, you entirely forget what you're about and only realise it sometime later when full lucidity returns to you and you find yourself wondering (or even marvelling at) what the hell you were doing so thoughtlessly just now. It's like drifting off into a daydream and then coming to your senses again when something jogs your memory, usually by unknowingly interacting with other people in the dream and only realising it afterwards. The mere presence of other people in the dream usually seems to be the reason for this, as if they, for some reason, directly affect your level of lucidity.

Nevertheless, hang around long enough, even in this third and more difficult area of dreaming, and your lucidity eventually increases again and stabilises enough to again go for a wander around in order to explore.

Level four is the full lucid dreaming scenario and a situation in which anything can (and does) happen, where you experience every conceivable combination and situation that you can ever remember encountering in any of your unconscious, random dreams before. Having already slowly adjusted and acclimatised yourself down through the previous three levels, it doesn't take too long to adjust to the slightly extra difficulty of this fourth. The grip you have already gained and tightened over your lucidity in the previous easier levels stands you in good stead in this fourth one, which does not really differ that much from the previous three, other than in terms of just how well populated it is in comparison.

There is one other 'level' that I've recently discovered which might be more correctly labelled level zero than level five. It is a very strange place indeed in terms of awareness, whereby one is neither completely awake nor in a lucid dream. It is a kind of 'in-between' or middle ground position that's very hard to describe, something of which I was not even aware at the time because I was so keen on only experiencing a lucid dream. Since lucid dreaming was my sole objective initially, I didn't realise that I was passing through this area every time on my way into the dreams, and it's very peculiar and interesting, along with providing access to some of the most exciting experiences yet in all of this. For example, after many minor but incredibly lucid dreams, at one point I found myself in this middle-ground area, a kind of 'midway point' between waking and dreaming. To my subjective left there was what can only really be described as a being a floating bubble surrounded by darkness which contained some sort of an illuminated scene, and to the right was my body asleep (or at least lying down) in bed. I didn't initially know what I was doing there, only that at the time I didn't want to wake up yet; I wanted to lucid dream some more. So, I kind of deliberately stepped towards the bubble with the scene in it and, before you know it, I was right inside it in a fully-fledged lucid dream. Moreover, from this perspective I could still see both that midway point and myself lying in bed at the same time. How very strange! Ignoring all this, I decided to remain in a lucid dream, after all, that *was* my original purpose for being there in the first place. So I abandoned what appeared to be the other two available options and plunged right into the dream, all the better to explore it. However, in spite of all the things I did in that particular dream on that occasion, throughout those experiences, I could still see that midway point and also see, and sort of feel, myself lying in bed at the same time. They were just kind of farther away or more distant from me than the lucid dream I'd chosen to be in and I could somehow sense all this, resolving, as the whole session ended, to explore this in greater detail the next time, which I did. Moreover, having in the meantime experienced otherwise fairly ordinary lucid dreams aplenty, it is this fifth level (or level zero if you prefer) of dreaming that is currently holding my full attention because it's absolutely fascinating. I am almost at a total loss about how to describe it, let alone explain it. It is really the weirdest and most interesting thing of the lot – a position (or place, then) in awareness whereby apparently lucid dreaming becomes only *one* – albeit distinct – option among many. I don't know as yet what all the other options besides lucid dreaming are, but entering into lucid dreaming or waking up in the daily world are definitely two of them. But there's more, a kind of unexpected bonus that I know for sure doesn't ever seem to come up in a DILD.

Currently, I can't profess to know what it is exactly, or even what it truly represents in terms of extending one's awareness into other areas, other than that, from this (midway) position lucid dreaming becomes what it needs to become if people are genuinely going to explore and map it in some kind of bona fide, useful, systematic fashion. Under these circumstances lucid dreaming truly becomes a matter of choice and on demand.

Changing Dreams

I'd like to write a little here about changing dreams once one is already in a lucid dreaming state. This is something that was discovered entirely by accident and which I'll write about and attempt to describe in the first person since this seems the simplest and most direct approach. For example, after several more relatively uneventful experiences in, what appeared to be, an empty orange room on the first level, and with my confidence beginning to rise, I felt that I was perhaps ready for something a little more adventurous. Immediately, the idea of seeing other people in the dream and of being able to interact with them to some extent came to mind.

Having absolutely no clue as to how to proceed, I closed my eyes in that dream and began to repeat out loud over and over, "I want to see people, I want to see people." The almost immediate result of this was suddenly to feel myself falling irresistibly asleep in that dream and waking up again moments later in a completely different one, this time with people in it. I was totally shocked by this turn of events, but straightway I could feel that something had changed drastically. The steadiness and predictable calmness of the dream with the orange room had been replaced with something far busier and more vibrant. I looked around, I appeared to be in another room that was fully furnished and brightly lit as though with daylight. Several people were there, sitting on soft chairs in little groups, talking to each other. I looked around the room examining the furniture and décor, which all seemed fairly modern in style, layout and mood. There were even some attractive leafy green plants growing in a couple of carefully placed red clay pots that seemed to blend very nicely and fashionably with the rest of room, as though someone had put quite a lot of thought into decorating and arranging it.

However, there was also something very different about this dream compared to the one of the orange room, in that it was suddenly noticeably difficult to maintain my lucidity, which I could feel kind of wavering. I struggled for a moment to pull myself together and to dispel my faltering lucidity by shaking my head a couple of times and by exerting my will, something which appeared to have a positive effect as I felt my lucidity returning to me. It was strange, almost as if the mere presence of other people in my dream was distracting to me in some way or perhaps pulling me deeper into the dream, with the result that my lucidity and memory of what I was doing became impaired. What was completely easy to maintain in the empty orange room, required a much more conscious and deliberate attempt on my part to maintain in this one. I puffed and panted with the effort for a few moments and then, quite abruptly, I was fully lucid again, marvelling and pondering the remarkable difference existing between the two dreams.

My intuition was informing me that dreams with people in them exist at a 'deeper level' of dreaming than the other one with no one in them except me, at which point I spontaneously realised that there are, in fact, different levels to lucid dreaming. What was only an idea and a question moments before transformed into a seemingly undeniable and completely self-evident certainty before my very eyes. The ideas I was experiencing were more like fleeting images rather than thoughts proper. The revealed method of changing from one level to another was akin to that of falling asleep in the dream you're in and then waking up in another, something I hadn't even known about before that very moment.

The action of attempting to rally my fading lucidity was apparently now placing me in a position to be able to see once more (or rather, visualise) that midway point, which I also knew I could somehow just step right back into at a moment's notice should I wish to. However, feeling fully lucid again, and reassured by that, I turned my attention instead back to the room with people in it and again attempted to interact with them. I slowly looked at each person in turn, although no one seemed even to notice my presence. I didn't really know what to do. Everyone there was a stranger to me and so I kind of wished it was my own friends I was among instead of strangers, as though that fact might have made some difference. At this point I could feel myself falling back to sleep again in that dream with my vision becoming blurry as though my eyes were filled with tears. I experienced then a distinct sensation of slightly sinking as my blurred vision darkened to utter black. I knew I was falling asleep, I could 'feel' it, but the very next moment I woke up again somewhere else, this time in another but completely different room, this time one with only one person in it, who was apparently fast asleep in bed! I approached and saw that it was a young friend of mine, a young lady whom I knew in the waking world – and here she was, fast asleep.

I realised, of course, that my desire to see someone familiar had resulted in my changing dreams, and it was again noticeably more difficult than before to maintain my lucidity. I observed her for a while lying there quite comfortably in her bed and wondered what to do. I hadn't expected anyone to be asleep, which kind of threw me. I came closer to her and saw that it really was the person I thought it was and marvelled at the situation I was in. I also wondered if it was, in fact, the real person or just a dream image of her. I shook her gently by the shoulder to see if she'd wake up but nothing happened. I shook her a little harder, rocking her shoulders a little more firmly but still to no avail, she didn't even stir. Clearly, she just carried on sleeping. I could see her breathing. At this point I really didn't know what to make of it all but a kind of inner-voice coming from somewhere seemingly behind me that couldn't be seen, said, "You've really got to shake them hard." Without thinking twice I gave her really quite a firm shove, loudly calling her name, whereupon she moved in her sleep and turned over but didn't as yet awaken. I was worried now that, for some reason, I might actually be looking at and seeing the real person involved, and not only a dream image. I judiciously decided to leave well alone, making a mental note to come back to all this later. The real point of this story is an attempt to describe how it feels, once in lucid dreaming, to change dreams along with how it's done. Presumably there are other, perhaps even better, ways of accomplishing exactly the same thing, but that's just what happened (and happens) to me.

An altogether rather remarkable aspect of being awake in a dream is this almost intuitive understanding that seems to come out of nowhere and explain things and what they mean as they're occurring, or just immediately afterwards. For example, when I stated out loud my desire to see other people in my dream and felt myself falling asleep only to wake up in another one, this time a dream with people in, it was as though everything all suddenly slotted into place and made sense once it had occurred. I somehow *intuitively* understood what had happened and how, but only *after* it had occurred, the same thing happening after I voiced my desire to see someone familiar. I didn't know then I was going to fall asleep again and wake up in another dream in order to accomplish my intention, but immediately realised upon awakening in that new dream *exactly* what had just occurred and *why*. Obviously, this is something that happens to us in ordinary, random dreams as well, yet we never actually realise it at the time and just carry on, albeit in completely different situations sometimes. For example, our going (or transiting, then) from being in one place to another (e.g. from being in a house to suddenly standing in a park) without ever realising it and then just carrying on as though being in that park was completely expected and normal, but which is something that is (or readily becomes) quite apparent when lucid in the dream.

False Awakenings

As an experienced lucid dreamer using DILDs you may have already encountered false awakenings in the course of your exploring. These 'false awakenings' are something that I'm sure really only ever happen to DILD-doers, and are the sensation that one has woken up in the waking world after lucid dreaming, only to discover subsequently that one is still actually dreaming. The resultant jolt, or shock realisation of this is usually enough to *really* wake you up only, yet again, to realise before long that you're still dreaming. Apparently, some people experience a whole series of several such false awakenings in succession until, in the end, they no longer know for certain whether they're awake or still dreaming.

The first time this ever happened to me personally was many, many years ago while living in a kind of communal house. On that occasion I had gone to sleep as normal on one of the many mattresses and large armchairs in the main room and woke up several hours later. Everything was more or less the way it should have been with all the same people still there from the night before. I got up from my bed just as the doorbell rang. Someone else in the house answered it, accompanied by the sound of squeals of delight and recognition from several of the people standing just inside the front door because Sonia, one of the girls staying there who had been missing for three or four days, had finally turned up. We'd all been quite concerned for her whereabouts and to see her back safe and sound had us all flocking around her to welcome her home. Everyone was trying to talk to her at once.

"Where have you been?"

"What happened to you?"

"Are you alright?"

Everyone was relieved to see her back safe and sound again at the house, only to discover that she'd apparently been remanded in jail on some minor charge of shoplifting and had only just been let out. However, as I stood there along with the others I began to feel a little odd. At first it was like feeling ever so slightly dizzy, and then, with growing consternation, I noticed some white and purple stripes appearing right on the periphery of my vision. I gently shook my head several times to try and dispel it, which almost seemed to work – except that each time I did this it went away and came back even more pronounced than before. By now I definitely felt rather woozy, and as I watched in a kind of stunned, and growing, silent horror, the purple and white stripes pushed their way further and further in towards the centre of my vision until that was all I could see. For a little while everything was just purple and white zigzagging stripes and lines. I felt then like I was falling backwards in slow motion and I can remember thinking quite rationally that this must be what fainting was like. All of a sudden I opened my eyes again only to find myself back in my bed and sitting up just as I had done the first time. I wasn't really frightened exactly because somehow I knew, without any shadow of a doubt, that 'this' time I was really awake! I sat up, amazed and perplexed. I looked around. Everything was as it had been the first time. The same people were there along with everything else, and just as I leapt up preparing to tell all and sundry about what had happened to me there was the sound of something coming through the letterbox and instead I quickly ran into the hall to find a plain blue envelope lying face-down on the mat which, I just *knew*, contained a letter from Sonia in prison! The most remarkable aspect of this entire episode was that it *was* a letter from our lost friend Sonia who *was* indeed being held on remand on some minor charge of shoplifting. The oddest thing about the whole experience, which I eventually later told and then retold to my friends and acquaintances was that, for several days afterwards, I was semi-convinced that the 'reality' of the first experience of wakening was such that I couldn't now totally discount the possibility of it ever happening to me again at any moment. It was a very strange and haunting feeling that lingered for several weeks, although, needless to say, it never did occur again; it was, however, still a great story to relate to people at dinner parties for quite a while afterwards. Since it was never repeated, however, it eventually became something buried and forgotten about over time and it was only years later that I came to understand that these so called 'false awakenings' are, in fact, a fairly common experience among lucid dreamers using the DILD method.

However, this never seems to happen with WILDs. I think this is because with WILDs you are awake from the start and fully realise that this is so and consequently there is never any confusion. I could of course be wrong, but as far as my own experience is concerned, false awakening only happens to those dreamers using DILDs in order to gain access to their lucid dreams, which doesn't occur when WILDing.

The Midway Point

We return now to an amazing and rather illuminating aspect of lucid dreaming the WILD way, something which appears to be totally lacking in DILDs but ever-present almost from the beginning with WILDs; the ability to be in several places at once. This is an automatic aspect of lucid dreaming from the point of view of having entered into them being already fully awake. I am at a loss to explain this fully, apart from the observation that it is a seemingly consistent feature of WILDing that is almost totally absent from DILDs; the very strange awareness of being in several places at once, either singularly or even all at the same time. This is an experience I find difficult to describe directly or accurately except, perhaps, in terms of what I have experienced personally and from which you may be able to draw your own conclusions.

For example, the first time I lucid dreamed in WILDs in any kind of prolonged manner I just so happened to be lying on my left side and didn't realise yet what a difference left-sided dreams would make as far as their content was concerned. While playing around with hypnagogia the dream began and, very abruptly, I found myself in an old orange painted room in some apparently abandoned building, an apartment that appeared to have been inhabited at some point in the past, yet the occupants had moved away leaving behind just bare floorboards and dust, cracked paint and the odd piece of wastepaper strewn around. The overall impression was that the place was deserted and that no one had been there for quite some time. (Symbolic or what?)

I was perfectly aware that I was dreaming and, not wanting the dream to end prematurely, I deliberately ignored the sudden jolt of the realisation that I was actually dreaming and walked about examining the room instead. However, my fears about accidentally dispelling the dream prematurely were unfounded because everything in the dream remained steady and clear no matter what I thought or did. My normal waking memory was also completely unimpaired; I could think perfectly clearly and, although I didn't really know what to do next, I was able to take the time to consider my next move carefully. In the meantime, I walked around the apartment from room to room examining things. The decor was just about the same in every room I visited, a kind of deep, dusty, faded orange colour on plain painted walls. Everything about it said old and deserted, yet even the dust in that place twinkled dimly with a kind of inner-light of its own. The most remarkable thing about it was the complete steadiness and seeming *realness* of everything I was seeing and touching. I examined myself and appeared to be just as real and solid as I usually knew myself to be and found myself casually dressed in jeans and a t-shirt.

After a while, I remembered reading somewhere of a dreaming technique whereby touching the tip of your tongue on the roof of your mouth while lucid dreaming was supposed to enhance your lucidity, and to that end I attempted to do so. Only what happened next was totally unexpected. I suddenly found myself firmly pressing my thumbs against the curled forefingers of my hands which had made a fist. The immediate effect of which was almost electrifying in terms of the increased clarity I then suddenly experienced! However, what I had thought was marvellously clear and sharp before paled to insignificance compared to what was happening now. The best way to describe it is that everything, myself included, literally lit up and sparkled with its own vibrant inner energy and colours. What had been rather drab and dull only moments before now suddenly glowed in almost scintillating rainbow colours that shocked me and made me step back a bit.

I marvelled at how I had intended to do one thing only to find myself doing something completely different, namely, pressing my thumbs instead of touching the tip of my tongue to the roof of my mouth. At which point, and with no warning whatsoever, I abruptly found myself lying back in bed, on my left side, in my darkened bedroom where I immediately noticed I was also pressing my thumbs against the curled fingers of my hands there too. I really didn't know what to think about this sudden, strange turn of affairs, but I remembered that what I was originally trying to do was to enhance lucidity by holding my tongue against the roof of my mouth and, quite logically, assumed that if I did so while I was still awake in bed, then maybe this would also transfer itself back into the dream. So, without changing my position at all, I did just that; I deliberately un-pressed my thumbs and instead held my tongue against the roof of my mouth. Without knowing how, the next thing I knew I was back in the same orange room as before, except now I was indeed touching the tip of my tongue against the roof of my mouth. Only it didn't seem to do anything at all; the sparkling colours had simply reverted back to drab and dull again, the tongue-trick disappointingly not appearing to have any effects at all upon lucidity. What I couldn't figure out, however, was how I had managed to be pressing my thumbs when I had originally intended to do something else altogether. I had sought a greater lucidity in the dream and achieved it, although not quite by using the method I'd set out to employ. I pondered on this for quite a while in the dream only to find myself suddenly back in bed still lying on my left side.

Dammit! I thought, realising quite clearly that my rather ponderous behaviour had just got me booted out of my very first prolonged lucid dream, only I could somehow tell that I wasn't yet fully awake in the usual sense. I was clearly lying in bed with my eyes closed and still hadn't moved or changed position at all, yet I could also still see the orange dream room floating like a bubble in the pitch dark just a few metres away. In fact, I seemed to be in a very strange place where I could clearly see both the lucid dream and myself lying in bed at one and the same time. At this point it only required a simple shift of focus to switch from one to the other. I wanted to know more about this strange place between waking and dreaming, but my original intention to have a lucid dream convinced me to go that way instead. I stared at the dream bubble to the left of me in which I could clearly see now what looked like buildings of some sort and stepped/leaned towards it. Instantly I was back in a lucid dream again only this time everything appeared to be at arm's length compared to the utter convincing reality of that initial orange room dream. I appeared to be in a modern and spacious garage of some sort. All the recognisable tools of the mechanic's trade were lying around either on the ground or on shelves, and I was looking at everything which still exhibited a very dreamlike quality in this dream as opposed to the utter reality of the first. That 'utter reality' effect was what I really craved again, only now everything was vague and seen as though I was only viewing it while still lying in bed or as if seen from a distance. I was definitely in the dream, and yet, I was still not quite in it like I was before, with everything somehow lacking that former convincing *realness*.

At this point a young man in clean, garage-type, light green overalls stepped out from a doorway and glanced briefly in my direction while walking towards what looked like a large lever standing four feet tall from the floor. He slowly pulled on that lever and, to my amazement, a circular area of about twelve feet all around me began to sink slowly into the ground with me still standing on it. I quickly realised that I appeared to be standing on some sort of an industrial elevator that was lowering me down to other levels of that building. Not knowing what to do I just stood there and watched as the ground slowly sank away below me and I descended with it. I watched several floors in succession pass me by as I went down until finally, I seemed to be at the bottom of a fairly long shaft that now towered above me several stories high. The platform I was standing on was definitely slowing down and apparently fitting itself into a large matching circular area where it was obviously going to stop, but I stepped off of it before it had time to dock fully with the ground. My sensation of the solid reality I had wanted had apparently returned to me at this level and I was truly back in the dream in the same concrete way I had been formerly. I glanced behind me at the elevator as it continued to slowly dock with the ground but deliberately ignored the dark space full of, what looked like, stars just below it. I was fully back in the lucid dream again and that was all I really cared to know.

There was no one else around. Beyond some swing doors I could see daylight and I walked towards it quickly finding myself outside in bright sunshine. I looked around. I was apparently out in the countryside with trees, hedges and fields all around me. I could see the blue sky above and the horizon in all directions. I could just feel the *reality* of it all, so real, in fact, that I doubted for a moment that I was still dreaming. I wanted, at that point, to prove to myself that I was indeed still dreaming and figured quite rationally that, if

I was really dreaming, then I should be able to just fly up in the air if I wanted to. With this in view I mustered all the strength and intent that I could and leapt up into the air to see if I could indeed fly, but the force with which I jumped must have been too much for I literally took off like a bullet and shot up into the air so fast and furiously that, before I even fully realised what was happening, I could clearly see the curvature of the earth and the blackness of space beyond. A blackness that then swallowed me whole as I continued to gain altitude, only to suddenly find myself back in bed again. I was completely nonplussed! Apparently, my overzealous and prodigious leap in that dream had taken me all the way out to waking. D'oh! I lay there awake, literally tingling all over from the jolt of waking up so fast, only again, I wasn't quite awake in the normal sense and was instead back at that same midway point between waking and dreaming. How strange!

Again, I could clearly see that bubble of a lucid dream hovering there in the dark nearby which appeared to be only a step or two away and slightly to my left. My resting body then appeared like another option but slightly off to my right, or rather, the option to be fully awake appeared to my right, even though I was completely aware of myself lying down in bed. This place between these two options was indeed very strange and I decided at that point to investigate further.

To my utter surprise, I quickly discovered that I was somehow able to hover at that midway point, being totally aware of myself lying down in bed, yet at the same time knowing that I wasn't fully awake in the normal sense. The option to regain full consciousness was like something that hovered ever so slightly to my right, just as the option to step straight back into that lucid dream seemed to hover ever so slightly to my left. Furthermore, I could apparently change or shift my point of view from one to the other and back again at will. In fact, at that moment the option to lucid dream appeared to be equal to the option to reawaken completely. In order to prove this to myself, I deliberately, and in full consciousness, stepped right back into the lucid dream, only this time the need to feel myself descend in an elevator was completely unnecessary because the dream I stepped into was exactly the same dream as before with the same feelings of solid reality. I was right back in a lucid dream and this time it had been completely effortless, merely the decision to do so being apparently enough to take me right back into it. Again, I was genuinely amazed at this sudden unexpected and unanticipated turn of events but, never having experienced any of this before, I assumed that this was probably all perfectly normal.

I looked around me and saw and noted all the things I had seen in the last dream, trees and rolling cultivated countryside that stretched to the horizon in all directions, added to which was the absolute certainty that I was right back in the exact same dream and place as before. Fascinating! At this point I noticed that I was also aware of myself still standing back at the midway point, and found that I could again shift my point of view back and forth between those two points of view. I could be exclusively in one or the other, yet, paradoxically, even in both at the same time, although when I did that – by which I mean experiencing both simultaneously – I noticed that the sharp clarity of either point of view was slightly dulled. It was while I was playing around with all this that I then became aware that I could also feel myself lying down in bed. With no effort on my part I found I could very easily shift back and forth between all three perspectives, with an ever so slight focusing on my part being enough to accomplish it.

The more I played around with it the easier it became, even to the point of being able to see, feel and experience all three places at the same time. Added now to which, a feeling of utter confidence began to take hold. Moreover, at this point I spontaneously realised that shifting back and forth like that had somehow completely erased all doubts and caution on my part. Nothing I had read or heard had prepared me for anything like this and, believe me, I'd read lots about lucid dreaming and thought I at least knew what to expect.

I liked the feeling I'd had while standing at the midway point. I enjoyed the sheer clarity of it and the warm feelings of calm confidence that came with it, and so I deliberately returned to that point again in order to examine it further. I realised then that all this shifting back and forth had also created in me a very strong sense of total detachment, so strong, in fact, that I was surprised by the intensity of it. I had already considered myself to be fairly detached before but this was something new and at a completely different level. In fact, it was almost frighteningly cold and distant in a way I'd never quite experienced before, yet at the same time a strong sense of unparalleled confidence grew out of that very detachment in a way that's hard to describe. This new detachment allowed me not only to do whatever I wanted to do at the time, but also provided me with the direct knowledge of exactly *how* to do it.

From then on, my ability to dream took on, and rose to, incredible proportions. I shan't, however, bore you with the details of the several other dream sequences that followed that I explored with utter facility and total abandon. The part I want to come to now concerns the final sequence of events that occurred *after* I had finally decided that I'd had enough of dreaming for now and chose to wake up.

The point here is that it wasn't really a conscious, rational decision as such on my part to finish dreaming; it was more like a decision that my body made for me by itself. Not that I felt fatigued or bored with it exactly, it was more like the feeling you experience while enjoying a really delicious meal to the point at which you suddenly realise that you simply cannot finish those last few lovely mouthfuls because you're feeling stuffed to the gills. In other words, my body suddenly informed me that I'd had enough and I kind of agreed, albeit reluctantly. Something, some part of me, an unfamiliar bodily sense was clearly suggesting 'that's enough for now and let's pack it in' and so I took that option.

It was early morning and I lay there on my side awake in bed for a few moments playing over in my mind the events of the night. All in all, it had not only been an incredible experience, but also an extremely instructive one. However, as I got up to make myself a cup of tea I noticed that the same powerful mood of utter detachment was still with me. In fact, I only thawed out by degrees over the next four or five hours. It was as though I couldn't actually think at all and could still see and know everything without having to think about it first in the usual sense. The waking world itself also looked slightly different from normal in a way that was difficult to define. I managed to make, and eat, a light breakfast of toast and tea without having a single thought about it. I felt kind of strange and rather unknown to myself but enjoyed the feeling immensely. Eventually, after several hours, there came a moment when everything just seemed to click back into place and I became recognisably myself again. I had mixed feelings of being glad to be fully myself once more but also slightly sad at the loss of that incredible and overpowering sense of detachment and freedom that went hand in hand with it.

I can now say that this hindsight is, and was, actually instrumental, not only to lucid dreaming itself the WILD way, but also to having and experiencing changes of awareness in general. Even two or three hours after waking I honestly felt that I knew everything there was to know about lucid dreaming, and other things too, but as that detachment wore off I noticed that complete knowledge of lucid dreaming also began to fade. The perceptual effects being like that of a thick velvet curtain that slowly descended between me and that silent *knowing* that had given me so much confidence and ability. The well-known and reported energising effects of having lucid dreamed still remained with me, however, for several days afterwards with my sense of well-being seemingly at an all-time high. I found myself literally dancing about with gusto and a relaxed ease that I'd only experienced on very few occasions in the past. I was high for days, I felt happy and carefree. I didn't need anything at all and, most surprisingly, not even any more lucid dreaming. Something in me, some yearning, had been completely satisfied by that initial extended experience that lasted for over five or more hours in all.

That detachment, that 'mood of the dreamer', was something that could only be genuinely acquired by the direct experience of lucid dreaming itself, even if only the once, being a particular feature of having WILDs. This is something you really need to experience for yourself in order fully to understand the depth, fullness and sheer beauty of it.

Lucid Dreaming on Demand

What if everyone could lucid dream any time they wanted to, literally as much as they want? Wouldn't that be something? That instead of there being only sixteen hours a day on average of conscious wakefulness, this were to be extended to, say, twenty hours per day or more, albeit with these 'extra' hours of wakefulness spent lucidly dreaming. Wouldn't this in some sense change the way people tend to think about themselves and the lives they're living? This eventuality is something we are currently safe from, however, because the DILD method doesn't really allow for such regularity in lucid dreaming. Moreover, given the rather hit and miss nature of DILDs, even experienced practitioners would likely count themselves fortunate indeed to lucid dream once, or at most twice a week.

I can remember a time not that long ago when I would have given my eye-teeth in order to lucid dream, just once a week, let alone twice! It would have actually been earth-shaking. Lucid dreaming twice a week? Wow! But you would have to be mightily dedicated with the DILD method to get anywhere near accomplishing such a thing. Moreover, those that did manage it would likely be considered total experts in their field.

Fun though they are, the problem with DILDs is that, although you repeatedly give yourself the command to awaken in a dream *before* falling asleep and maybe also continually practice giving yourself 'reality-checks', listening to low frequency sounds while going to sleep, consuming tons of potentially dangerous exotic vitamin supplements, even wearing flashing face masks, you'll find that the whole process is largely unreliable and that your lucid dreaming just doesn't happen on a regular enough basis ever to be anything more than a passing novelty.

However, after much practice at it, slowly, (and, oh boy, we are talking months or even years here!) the habit to awaken whilst already dreaming may eventually become established to such a degree that, after much wearying persistence, some people, with dedication, can begin to spend longer and longer periods of time consciously exploring the dreaming state and be able to consider themselves fairly decent lucid dreamers.

It *is* possible to learn to lucid dream the DILD way – eventually. The only drawback is the sheer amount of time and effort required to make even the slightest progress, not to mention the financial investment in all that fancy apparatus – seminars, workshops etc.! No wonder, then, that people, having heard about this ability of ours to lucid dream, are sufficiently motivated to maybe buy a book or two on the subject and follow up a few links on the internet, yet without really having the time and resources to spend months trying to implement it. For many, therefore, DILDs are just too hard to bother with!

So then, imagine now that you could somehow enter into a lucid dreaming state more easily, more readily and far more often, more than just once, or even twice, a week (this last being the holy grail of DILDs) or even more than three or four times a week, as often as you wish! And by this I mean being able deliberately and consciously to enter into a dreaming state at will *without* having first to fall asleep in the usual manner. In fact, far from remaining a hit or miss affair for the persistent and/or somehow talented few DILD-doers, lucid dreaming under such circumstances would begin to take on a whole new meaning altogether, something that demanded to be assigned a totally different order of importance. If everyone could lucid dream, literally as much as they pleased it would massively change things. It would substantially affect our waking lives. In which case, welcome to WILDs and to WILDing!

Thus far lucid dreaming has remained the sole proprietary of the persistent few using the incredibly difficult and unpredictable DILDs method. Consequently, the whole subject of lucid dreaming appears to belong to some kind of fringe movement that bears no apparent relevance to life in modern society. However, with WILDs all that would change!

Factor in the curious ability of virtually *anyone* to enter into a lucid dreaming state – at will – whenever they wanted to 'on demand' and surely one would eventually be forced to beg the question as to what is all this and why are we even able to do it in the first place?

Unfortunately, as yet, we don't appear to have many answers to this puzzling conundrum since the possibility of people being able to lucid dream 'at-will' actually raises more questions than it provides answers for; nor do we have anything in our society or history to account for it beyond either the ravings of the tiny few or the rather dismissive 'quirk of perception' theory of rational science.

The point is that if lucid dreaming can be invoked upon command, as in the case of WILDs, it can hardly be just a glitch or quirk of perception. There has to be more to it and a logical explanation must be discovered. It might even begin to resemble something (an otherwise innate ability) that *everyone* has in ready reserve but never bothers to use.

The big question is what *are* dream states really? Is falling asleep and dreaming all the same, or are there different levels of dreaming?

Consider equally what, if anything, the relevance of these so-called dreaming-states is to the apparatus of our perception of our daily surroundings? This final notion has considerably more far-reaching implications if, for example, it ever turned out to be that all states of awareness, including normal waking awareness, are all, in fact, perceptual states of dreaming.

PART 3 – ADVANCED TECHNIQUES

Additional Techniques for WILDs

Assuming that you are already familiar with WILDs to some degree, at least to the point that you can now easily lucid dream three or four times a week, there are some general variations to the procedure that should be noted. For instance, the side of your body on which you initially lie down to dream, left or right, for some reason produces remarkably different results in terms of the dream scenarios you'll typically encounter. A left-sided sleeping position, for example, more often results in a single scenario lucid dream, whereas a right-sided sleeping position tends to produce a series of dreams in which one hops from one lucid dream to another in fairly rapid succession. This is not something for which I have an explanation, other than to report that this consistently occurs for some unknown reason. Since these are still very early days indeed when it comes to mapping the lucid dreaming state, who knows, maybe *you* will be the one who finally understands it and will then be able to explain it to the rest of us.

Anyway, with left-sided dreams one is apparently very much in control of the dreaming situation from the outset, with the option of changing dreams. Everything from the left side in dreaming is smooth, thus making it the perfect starting off position for newbies to have their very first, real, full lucid dream. In left-sided lucid dreams you feel fully awake and aware in every respect, which gives you time to manipulate your next moves judiciously and to put into action any experiments you may have had in mind. It is, for example, the perfect situation in which the beginner can quickly become accustomed to having lucid dreams as they won't be thrown around too much. Others, more advanced, are able to experiment with voicing out loud any questions they may have about life, the universe and everything. (Please see the chapter on the 'Uses of Lucid Dreaming' for a fuller explanation of this particular phenomena and technique.)

While sleeping on the right side, the dreams seem to change all by themselves without any warning or choice on the dreamer's part. Do nothing other than observe in a right-sided dream and you will find yourself going (or hopping) from one lucid dream to another in quick succession. However, it is also possible, if and when you so wish, to 'get off' in any one particular dream of your choice anywhere along the way during the sequence and explore that particular dream scenario in greater detail. Right-sided lucid dreaming is very much like someone slowly flicking through a picture book. Do nothing other than observe and the dreams change from one to the next and then the next and so on, with the dreamer spending maybe only four or five minutes in each scenario before being moved on.

Left-sided dreams are, however, a completely different matter. For some (unknown) reason they are always far more stable and under one's complete control from the outset. Enter into lucid dreaming while lying down on your left side and you will experience a dreaming lucidity that's hard to match under any other circumstances. Everything on the left side is always clear and steady and doesn't morph spontaneously into anything else. You yourself also remain stable and the dreams encountered are never so complicated that you find yourself struggling to understand what's going on. In fact, in these dreams everything always seems completely self-explanatory. In left-sided dreams, you can wander around scenarios and explore to your heart's content. You can, seemingly, think completely clearly as normal, yet also remember who you are and what you are trying to do. In left-sided sleeping position dreams you are generally always yourself as you know yourself to be, making it the perfect situation in which to explore the experience of being in such an altered state of awareness.

In right-sided dreams, by contrast, the dreams themselves are far more complicated. You'll be presented with a series of often novel and very compelling dreaming situations that almost force you to interact with them. Lucidity is still full, as is full waking memory, but in these dreams there is no real volition as to what you'll be dreaming about or the situation you will find yourself in. Furthermore, the dreams themselves tend to change from one situation to another very quickly without giving the dreamer any time to adjust as you barely have time to get used to one novel dream scenario before being hurled off into another. Nevertheless, it is quite possible to 'get-off' this ride at any point and remain in that particular dream scenario for the duration of the session should you so wish. That is, assuming you are already aware of what is really happening, although deliberately changing dreams once having selected any particular scenario to explore doesn't appear to be an option. The session usually ends by eventually waking up from that particular dream once it's over.

The same can't be said, however, for left-sided dreaming wherein 'choice' appears to be a far greater feature of the whole thing with each dream session being entirely steady and stable to a point. In these dreams you can explore, experiment and change dreams (once you have learned to do so) virtually at will. Left-sided initiated dreams are readily amenable to conscious manipulation.

Adopting the sleeping position of lying either on one's front or back in this instance does not appear to have any particularly noticeable or discernible effect compared with that of lying on either side, other than perhaps a slightly longer time period involved in getting-off into dreaming itself. However, that might merely be something personal to me. There is indeed something 'different' about the resulting dreams from these prostrate and supine sleeping positions, just as there is a noticeable difference between dreaming on either side, but as yet I haven't been able to discover exactly what it is. Maybe some dreamer more capable than I will bring us the answer to this and many other curious dream-state conundrums in the very near future.

Since lucid dreaming is a new and relatively unexplored frontier in the understanding of consciousness, the sky is clearly the limit for any would-be pioneer to forge ahead into unknown territory and bring back some hitherto unknown gems of awareness. Exploring and probing outer space is something that calls for heroes with wills of iron to accomplish, whereas the exploration of inner space is open to virtually everyone who wants to attempt it. Believe me, once you start having lucid dreams and experiencing the sheer wonder and excitement of them, and of you yourself being in them and the opportunities this provides, you'll certainly want to discover things about lucid dreaming that can then be shared with, and appreciated by, others.

Techniques for DILDs

Dream-induced lucid dreams (DILDs) are what I'd call 'classic lucid dreams', a currently scientifically inexplicable phenomena whereby right in the middle of an ordinary dream you either suddenly, or by degrees, become aware that you are dreaming. DILDs is definitely old-school as far as I'm concerned, especially when compared to the sheer rapidity, novelty and instant clarity of WILDs.

This being book mainly about WILDs, I'm accordingly not going to go into too much detail about lucid dreaming from the DILD side of things, beyond maybe providing a brief outline of the whole general process for beginners. Especially considering that probably 99% of the information available out there on lucid dreaming, both in books and on the internet, is about DILDs and hardly anything else.

The basic concept behind DILDs is to train oneself to go to sleep as normal and to then become conscious again later when you're already having a dream. A nearly impossible thing to achieve per se, but which is made possible through a combination of various applied techniques, coupled with a really prolonged, prodigious effort.

For example, using 'reality checks' to train oneself during waking consciousness to regularly check the reality of one's surroundings by asking yourself 'am I dreaming or not?' and then testing to see if it's true. The idea behind this being, that once you've cultivated this 'reality-check' as a regular habit in yourself, then one of the times you ask yourself this you may well discover that this time you are, in fact, dreaming and can then begin to act accordingly. It's all rather convoluted but it does eventually work. Sustaining the shock of suddenly realising you are dreaming (there's that

'Yikes!' factor) being something else again that takes much practice to perfect. Practice that's extremely rare if using only the DILD method!

The standard DILD method demands that just before going to sleep you repeatedly give yourself the command to wake up later in a dream. This is a bit like tapping yourself on the head eight times to make yourself wake up at 8.00 a.m., something which apparently works for some people.

Or, you could try using a combination of both approaches, or any one or more of several other available methods. The main thing being to really want to have lucid dreams and to persist for long enough with any of the DILD methods involved until in the end it begins to happen for you. (I initially spent months falling asleep intoning to myself that "I want to lucid dream! I want to lucid dream!" over and over with no appreciable effect whatsoever! What a disappointment and waste of time!)

There are also 'techno' helps available, in the form of flashing lights worn as a face mask while going to sleep, this perhaps coupled with particular audio frequency sounds that have reputedly been proven to help generate the appropriate brain waves for lucid dreaming. Something which, all in all, sounds a bit too clumsy to me, involving a lot of faffing about and pre-preparation.

Personally, I think the whole DILDs thing is currently too tricky and necessarily involves a lot of faffing about. Thus I would say to anyone wishing to have a lucid dream, don't bother with DILDs at all and just go directly to the far more straightforward WILDs method. The results of which can be depended on from very early on in the process. I mean, why wait forever on a DILD when you can almost certainly have your very first lucid dream session within maybe only the next month or less via WILDs?

There is a ton of information on the internet about lucid dreaming, solely from the DILD point of view, together with all the mystique and sophism generally connected with it, for anyone that's interested. DILDs are mysterious by nature because usually the whole process of entering into dreaming is hidden right up until you actually find yourself in one. This is in stark contrast to WILDs, in which the whole process is revealed right from the outset and is mostly self-evident to anyone experiencing it right from the very first time.

DILDs are hard to do! And there's no fun involved in them for months until they start producing. They never did produce anything for me personally and thus I grew bored after several months of experiencing absolutely nothing. So bored, in fact, that I eventually began to experiment with the hypnagogia which accidentally resulted in my first WILD. Eureka! I think was my reaction when, on my very next session, I managed to repeat the experience. I haven't even attempted a DILD ever since!

As an added note to this, rather interestingly, after months of going WILD (I certainly did, heh) and lucid dreaming virtually every night (woo!) the few times I did actually fall asleep during the relaxation practices instead of going WILD, I later experienced a spontaneous DILD and become awake right in the middle of a strange and rather disturbing dream. The shock and realisation rocked me to my foundations as it slowly dawned on me that I was dreaming. What scared me the most was the fact that I couldn't sense my sleeping body or the midway point as usual, so I logically thought I was dead.

I guess I felt a little sad for a while contemplating all this; sad to have died and to be now facing some new reality, which was also a surprise to still be experiencing anything at all (laughs!). Only, of course, I wasn't dead, I was only DILD-doing and wasn't used to it! A marked feature of DILDs is apparently the express lack of awareness of one's sleeping body and that of the midway point. Subsequent DILDs confirmed this. Just why this resulting difference in awareness exists between the two different methods is unknown. But I'd certainly love to know.

One thing I can say, however, is that there is a distinct feeling of comfort (or reassurance) from still being able to sense one's sleeping body and/or that midway point. This is something seemingly lacking in DILDs but always present in WILDs. No one can yet explain why this is the case. So far, lucid dreaming certainly raises more questions than answers.

The Philosophy of lucid dreaming

"So what's the answer? That's what I keep asking myself
– what's it all about? Know what I mean?"
~ Michael Caine, *Alfie* (1966)

Until now this book has been a strictly technical manual of sorts, a very simple and straightforward 'how to do it' the WILD way, similar, perhaps, to just about any off-the-shelf DIY magazine for the aspiring home carpenter or motor mechanic.

The purely pragmatic aspects of WILDs are such, and so few in number, that the subject readily lends itself a simple format. To experience a WILD apparently requires very little effort or skill beyond that of merely mentally preparing oneself to have one, and then persisting with the suggested technique until it succeeds.

The mystique surrounding the whole subject of lucid dreaming has, until now, solely been a by-product of the sheer difficulties involved in initially producing them via a DILD and then reproducing them on any kind of regular basis using such methods. Undeniably, then, WILDs make lucid dreaming rather easy and readily accessible.

The method to 'induce' a WILD in itself is as straightforward and uncomplicated as, say, changing a fan belt or a spark plug is for the home mechanic; so much so, that just about anyone with even an iota of logical reasoning can very quickly and easily learn how to do it. If WILDs makes lucid dreaming so readily available, why then, with only very little practice, is it so universally easy to lucid dream on such a regular basis? What is it really all about and is there a philosophy, as such, to lucid dreaming?

I'm not sure that there currently is one, at least not one that hasn't been appropriated or fabricated by some strange cult or another and incorporated into a meaning entirely of their own, regardless of whether this apparent inherent ability of ours to lucid dream truthfully belongs there or not.

So, is there a meaning to lucid dreaming? By which, of course, I mean; is there perhaps some creditable reason or purpose behind being able to do so? Or is this rather odd and ostensibly unexplained phenomenon, as science suggests, merely some physical or psychological glitch of perception? One that, with practice, people are able to learn and exploit for the purposes of mere entertainment, but which means little else beyond that?

What, for example, would it mean to the way people lived and viewed their daily lives if, instead of always just having ordinary random dreams, it suddenly became possible for just about anyone to enter into a variety of lucid dreaming states at will? Wouldn't that eventually affect people's entire outlook on life and the way they tend to see themselves living it? Something which, on the surface of things, seems like a reasonable enough question to ask, especially considering that, from the point of view of rational science, we shouldn't even be able to do lucid dreaming at all.

Ordinary dreams are still little understood by medical science and are currently accepted as a by-product of consciousness, the result of a kind of 'standby' mode that the brain enters into during sleep instead of shutting down completely. Something that is, perhaps, utilised to explore unconsciously novel or unfamiliar neural pathways encountered during waking that the cognitive part of the brain goes over and rehearses, which results in us having dreams. The physical body apparently even secretes amino acids specifically designed to inhibit movement whilst we are asleep, lest people inadvertently act out their dreams.

We need to dream, but where exactly does this ability to lucid dream fit into the grand scheme of things? Current understanding suggests that the physical need for sleep, plus that of REM sleep (Rapid Eye Movement, the period during which we dream) in particular, is pretty much universal across a wide spectrum and variety of organisms. Nearly all animals dream. We've all, for example, seen dogs whimpering and making running movements during their sleep that are obvious reactions to dreams. Sleep itself is even more universal across species than dreaming is, as nearly every species exhibits some form of resting state wherein the creature's metabolic rate slows considerably. Such 'resting' seemingly restores their depleted vitality, or at least conserves it. In other words, from hibernating bears to humming birds, an uncertain but definite kind of conservation of energy appears to exist in many forms, apparently to compensate for either the regular, short period nights when creatures can no longer see to hunt for food, to longer winter periods wherein hibernation was deemed evolution's most efficient solution for the seasonal scarcity of available resources. Life, apparently, exists and evolves along a knife's edge wherein energy is seemingly always at a premium rather than being plentiful. The fact that a lot of nature's work goes into energy conservation is self-evident but why many creatures also need to dream during their resting state in order to become revitalised is perhaps less clear. Studies have proved that depriving animals of the REM sleep, in which they typically dream, eventually renders them confused and ineffective during waking consciousness, and in many cases even deranges or kills them.

For example, without REM sleep we humans apparently just wither and waste away, both physically and mentally. It is as though such people haven't slept at all and exhibit many of the symptoms of sleep deprivation, even though they may have indeed physically slept for hours. It would seem, therefore, that REM sleep alone, along with the dreams that accompany it, is the key to obtaining the rest we so badly need.

One rather hilarious example of this was indirectly provided by a UK Big-Brother-type reality TV show. The broadcasters needed something different to maintain a waning public interest in such shows, at which point some bright spark apparently came up with the idea of gathering together a dozen or so willing subjects (or victims, as the case may be, heh!) who would allow themselves to be completely deprived of sleep for the duration of the show while being watched by the public as they presumably became increasingly confused and fell apart. (What will they think of next?) An entirely unexpected crunch came only a few days into the show when it was suddenly announced that the participants were all going to be allowed to sleep for ninety minutes every so often on the grounds that some of them were actually becoming psychotic! (Probably must have seemed like a cute idea at the time, heh?) Dreaming isn't just a side effect of sleeping – nor merely that of our minds doing some sort of housekeeping while we rest – but an absolute necessity for our well-being, without which all the sleep in the world can't compensate for!

This is kind of odd since it raises the question of why dreaming is so necessary for us to feel revitalised as opposed to just sleeping for several hours. Could it be true, therefore, that we really only sleep for hours and hours just to have several accumulated minutes of REM sleep? In which case, do we sleep only to dream?

Let us also consider that, from nature's point of view, every part of us serves some necessary functional purpose. Legs are used to stand upright, feet are used to stand those legs upon, hands are used to grasp and arms to give us reach and so on. Everything about us (and all creatures, for that matter) is entirely functional in design. Any seemingly redundant organs in the human body (we have two kidneys instead of only one, for example) being capable of fulfilling some crucial role or another should the need arise. An obvious exception to this is the human appendix, which dates back to a time in history when our ancient vegetarian ancestors, apparently, had a far longer digestive tract in order to help them digest copious amounts of vegetable matter. This much longer digestive system must have been altered somewhere along our evolutionary line as the branch of great apes we derive from began to eat increasingly more meat and cooked foods, so much so that a longer gut was no longer required and slowly reduced in length over, what must have been, vast periods of time in order for nature to evolve such drastic anatomical changes.

Evolution isn't, generally speaking, wasteful. Necessary parts slowly evolve into being as an adaptation to a changing environment and/or if deemed to have some kind of survival value to them. If something is no longer required it gradually devolves. This suggests that nature only really ever constructs and builds upon that which is actively required in order to minimally function.

The point here is that our ability to lucid dream appears to be homogeneously universal in that just about anyone is able to do it, regardless of age, education or background. In other words, lucid dreaming appears to be an entirely innate ability that requires only the intention to use it in order to bring it into full availability and operational use, almost as though it's something everyone should already know about and use. Only it's not.

Perhaps this is because somewhere in our history, (and I'm really only speculating here) it used to be more prevalent but gradually fell into disuse and became forgotten about until only the occasional village shaman or medicine man remembered anything about it. The only remnant of it that remains today consists of the standard, unconscious, nonsensical dreams that everyone, without exception, experiences on a daily basis. Dreams are something that people typically ignore unless they have a particularly vivid or scary dream, or have them analysed by psychologists for their subconscious meanings. That's basically as far as dreams and dreaming go in the rational world. The only slight exception is a small, but growing, number of people who have recently become interested in lucid dreaming if only as a kind of highly stimulating alternative form of recreation. (Which it certainly can be if that's all someone is looking for.)

However, even with such a small agenda as the above, just the practice of lucid dreaming alone seems to call into question the very nature of awareness in general, and it becomes increasingly apparent, even to someone who's not looking for it, that the nature of our awareness and perception has much more to it than we ever rationally suspected, possibly even massively so.

It's actually very odd when we begin to examine the whole process of sleeping, something which is taken completely for granted, if only because we've just always done it! And as far as most people are concerned, that's the end of the story. However, what if we choose to question it?

What if we examine this process of sleep and sleeping again, instead of just accepting it? What if we dare to question this absolute need to pass-out on a daily basis totally against our will? Especially considering that having dreams appears to be the chief goal of the whole process, rather than just that of the physical downtime required to recharge ourselves physically.

The point is that sleep is so commonplace, and dreams generally so vague and difficult to remember, that eventually we come simply to accept it and meekly acquiesce to sleep's demands. Large areas of our lives are given over entirely to doing so, even to the point that whole industries are totally dedicated to helping everyone to sleep as comfortably as possible.

Accordingly, if people could in any way reduce this involuntary downtime without any detriment to their health, then I don't doubt many would be only too happy to do so. However, the dicta of this absolute need to sleep demand a whole rigmarole of associated procedures (or rituals) singularly designed to place one into the position whereby one can, quite unconsciously, snatch a few moments of REM sleep.

The singular lack of information on this need, not only to sleep, but also to dream, means that we must disregard everything we think we know about the subject and start over with a complete re-examination of the entire process. This might just result in a better understanding of how it all works rather than meekly acquiescing to a process we otherwise take absolutely no conscious part in beyond just letting it happen. From nature's perspective, what, if anything, has dreaming got to do with everyday waking life that makes it compulsory?

The same can be said for lucid dreaming and everything we think we might already know about that subject and the many conclusions people have come to concerning it. In which case we should probably set accepted understanding aside and start from zero, collecting and collating evidence, the better to assess and understand what's really occurring during sleep, and why. Next, with a greater understanding of that process, we might even be able to take an active hand in it rather than just leaving it all to function on some unconscious default autopilot, as is mostly the case with the lucid dreams engendered by DILDs.

Do animals have lucid dreams too? I think they probably do, possibly even as much as we humans do, which is to say probably not very often. The chances are they have ordinary dreams, same as us, although with them it's always going to be an involuntary affair. Thus, by default, we humans mostly dream as animals do; unconsciously.

On the other hand, maybe it's entirely the other way around and all animals except human beings actually have lucid dreams every time they dream, dreams which are just as real to them as waking reality because they have no intellectual ability to discern any difference between them. Thus nature's paralysing amino acids might even make some sense insofar as this is simply nature's way of protecting us from our absolute need to dream.

Setting aside the many different cultural and religious connotations that have been added to dreams and lucid dreaming over long periods of time, many of them confusing and contradictory, maybe it is time to put all the current data aside and start observing and collecting anew.

To arrive at a more accurate assessment, any subsequent data we now collect should be based entirely upon the experience itself rather than trying to reconcile it to one potentially wacky idea or another that already exists, scientific or otherwise. While we have yet to come up with any definitive answers, we do find that an acute awareness and observation of the process of dreaming and having dreams is, in itself, quite revealing in many ways. It highlights a very specific use and application of our whole general apparatus of perception, often with direct implications about the way we use and apply it in our daily waking awareness too. Apparently, this is because the apparatus we use in perceiving and modelling both our waking and dream worlds are one and the same, lucid or otherwise. One appears to be a reflection of the other and vice-versa!

This brings us to the two types of lucid dreaming involved; DILDs and WILDs, each method standing in stark contrast to the other in terms of approach and accessibility although, in many instances, the results are inevitably the same. However, the marked differences between the two methods also highlight aspects of each other that might otherwise go unnoticed and remain unexamined if there was nothing with which to compare each method.

For example, with DILDs, the process itself of entering into a lucid dream is obscured by the need to fall first into an otherwise quite ordinary dreamless sleep, only becoming lucid later once an ordinary dream begins, often hours later. I feel that this whole approach perpetuates a situation that remains largely unchallenged as the very infrequency and usual vagueness of the dreams engendered by DILDs have the distinct tendency to keep the whole subject shrouded in mystery rather than clarifying anything. The best even an expert DILD dreamer can expect is to lucid dream every time he attempts to do so, albeit without ever really knowing how he actually does it. If DILDs were the only option open to us then surely that would be good evidence for the whole affair being merely some form of glitch of perception? However, the fact that DILDs can be superseded by the more fully aware process of WILDs, wherein one 'quite consciously' chooses whether or not to lucid dream, tends to suggest other alternatives. The 'fully conscious' and systematic exploration of another type of reality altogether for one, and the fully conscious exploration of an altered state without the use of drugs, being another. With WILDs the complete opposite situation prevails to that of DILDs. We enter into them fully conscious and awake, resulting in incredible clarity and stability of the lucid dreams, so that the whole process of lucid dreaming itself stands revealed from start to finish.

With DILDs one is left with the vague feeling that lucid dreaming is possibly something of great potential, only one doesn't know exactly what or the how beyond the fact that it works. Such questions and answers don't leap out at us when dreaming via DILDs, perhaps because we're not always fully conscious and alert enough in them to ask such questions anyway.

The same cannot be said of WILDs, however. Everything that occurs during a WILD seems to make clear and apparent sense all on its own. The dreamer almost immediately becomes cognisant of lacking some kind of deeper background knowledge, experience and/or perhaps missing cultural reference point that would lend some clearer purpose to it all beyond that of surface entertainment and novelty value alone. In dreaming virtually anything is possible, especially if the person doing the dreaming is fully conscious and aware of their situation, as with WILDs.

At first, probably everyone is overwhelmed by lucid dreaming in any form since it's such an energising, novel and invigorating experience that is virtually impossible to resist. Initially a little cavorting is perfectly understandable, but with experience the question inevitably arises; well, how come everyone else hasn't been doing this all along too?

This is where my own inquiry began, namely, upon finding a far more practical and wholly more predictable way into lucid dreaming. As previously mentioned, I'd perforce had a little fun only to end up eventually right back in this very same place wondering why is it possible to do this so very easily and to have never known about it. The innate ability to lucid dream, apparently, had been reduced to that of mere unconscious random dreams that were only ever occasionally remembered because I was always less than wide awake in them.

It still haunts me today that there doesn't appear to be a good reason for lucid dreaming but, unlike the human appendix, this ability hasn't atrophied into some sort of vestigial remnant but remains with us intact, entire and complete, albeit never fully utilised.

So okay, it's not that difficult to accept that we dream in order to refresh ourselves – but we've apparently settled for the very minimum default value of it, even though we surely have the proven ability to plug into the much greater energising source of lucid dreaming.

This brings us to another noteworthy point; that another emerging but undeniable fact about lucid dreaming is that even the slightest contact with the lucid dreaming state results in what can only be called a thorough refreshing of whatever it is that makes us feel tired in the first place. Effectively a mere forty-five or ninety minutes of 'lucid' dreaming is noticeably more physically restoring than a whole night's worth of ordinary sleep and dreams. I initially attributed this to an adrenalin rush released by having such an exciting experience, with just small amounts of lucid dreaming seemingly more than making up in terms of energy for a whole night of sleep. Although even that doesn't quite describe the result, in that after a lucid dreaming session one feels bursting with a surplus of energy that translates into an overall feeling similar to that of glowing health. This energised mood usually lasts for around three or four days before gradually fading away, a sensation, I might add, that one experiences from one's very first ever lucid dreaming session.

The experience itself is sufficient in that some kind of 'internal' understanding takes place which may or may not be verbalised in cogent rational terms, a clear case of the experimental versus the experiential. This inability to describe lucid dreaming, however, is no barrier to experiencing more of it. In fact, the very opposite is true in that too much rationality and reasoning whilst lucid dreaming is actually a sure fire way to get one's self booted right out of the dreaming state altogether, although with practice one eventually learns to strike the right balance. This is perhaps similar to standing midway along the length of a seesaw in that, once balanced, small movements either way can easily tip everything in that direction unless consciously counterbalanced and is something that can only be learned with practice.

Starting off as we are, inexperienced explorers crossing into a relatively unexplored frontier, only time and effort will map and/or identify certain common features of the dreaming state upon entering into it, the better maybe to signpost the way into and through it to fellow explorers coming along behind. What we need to explore and map this new area of experience and perception properly is daring, gutsy people who will have the time and motivation slowly to push back the boundaries of these other states of awareness maintained during sleep (if it's actually considered to be sleep at all) in which we can soberly function. This is something that has been occurring in just about every field of human existence, as people intelligently probe and explore the world around them. The nature of the human psyche and our potential as creatures of perception is no different from any other endeavour, in that small discoveries sometimes go on to yield huge mines of new information about ourselves and the amazing world around us.

For example, the human race has been exploring outer space, a very interesting but incredibly expensive affair, one that is certainly beginning to reveal something of the sheer scale and size of the universe. But what about inner space, which is possibly even larger and has so far been rather difficult to explore? The feeling during lucid dreaming is that there's far more to it than that of being just another playground. The truth is that we don't really know anything yet about the dreaming state beyond mere rumour and superstition.

Whatever you do with it, the fact is that the practice of lucid dreaming eventually begins quite naturally to impinge upon one's daily waking awareness in ways that are difficult to explain. The wonder of lucid dreaming is somehow gradually passed across to ordinary waking awareness too, in which case it ceases to be ordinary anymore at all, and indeed becomes extraordinary in the extreme. This alone warrants its exploration, if only for the way it ultimately deepens one's perception and appreciation of the wider waking world and that of ourselves being alive in it.

The rest is only a matter of comparing notes and experiences, which are all open to interpretation and cross-referencing for any common denominators, particularly that of entering into and out of the dreaming state itself and the various options one is presented with along the way, of which lucid dreaming is apparently only one.

It is at the point, where lucid dreaming crosses over into waking awareness and vice-versa, that it really all becomes fascinating, the full scope of which goes beyond that of this little 'how to do it the WILD way' book alone. Suffice then to outline some of the current observations, leaving the detail to be filled in and confirmed or debunked by younger, more able and agile minds than my own.

I can report, for example, that the nature of knowledge per se is different under the circumstances of lucid dreaming as it's very strange to be standing in a particular position in awareness, where it then becomes possible to step consciously into and out of a lucid dreaming situation at will. The action of doing this 'stepping' is a state of awareness that comes to you in and of itself, in and at the very moment it's required, and not beforehand. It's not a state of awareness, please understand, that one carries around in one's head, for example, and yet it's always right there exactly when you need it. In the dream reality (or state) one knows nothing in advance and everything at the moment.

Everything during the time of WILDing is seemingly self-explanatory and remains with you afterwards. However, exactly *how* you accomplished it begins to fade after a while, particularly after waking up in the waking world wherein, for quite some time afterwards, everything that occurred and how you did it, remains very clearly in view but gradually fades away. It is almost as though a dark curtain slowly descends on one's memory of the finer details of the whole experience as waking concerns and pursuits again rise to the fore.

The only way I've personally managed to maintain that awareness without it all fading away is, upon waking, to sit immobile almost as if in meditation so as to delay fully engaging with the normal actions of the waking world. Things such as getting up, dressing and maybe making a cup of tea for breakfast which, although not complex tasks, typically engage one's attention and are instrumental in bringing that curtain of forgetfulness right down until only a vague memory of your dreaming knowledge/awareness remains.

Oddly enough, the same situation also prevails in the dreaming world. The direct memories of the things one normally thinks about and does during waking also undergo a similar process whereby they typically fade from view or become noticeably suspended to some extent. This produces the effect, for example, of having prepared questions ready to ask upon entering into dreaming only to forget them immediately and almost in entirety upon doing so because they all now seem somewhat rather asinine. The point is that the kinds of things one thinks about in dreaming are not the same as those in waking and vice-versa. It is, however, entirely possible to bring full waking memories and planned experiments into lucid dreaming. It's just that to do so takes an inordinately concentrated effort, plus that of a certain amount of determination in order to carry them out, when the direct feeling and impulse at the time is mostly one of just immediately forgetting about all that 'stuff' and getting on with the business of dreaming instead. Likewise when waking, the only way I've personally found to remember the finer points of the sessions with any degree of accuracy afterwards is to write them down in detail immediately upon waking.

It's the strangest thing, but ever since starting to have lucid dreams, or rather the WILD version of them, my entire outlook on life, and of myself living it, has gradually changed. Certainly, previously rather fixed ideas have all but crumbled away under their impact, accompanied by a bewildering array of startlingly new and emerging ideas taking their place; so much so that it has even caused me to question many of our basic premises about who and what we really are and what we are all doing here. Lucid dreaming intuitively feels like discovering the tip of a proverbial iceberg in terms of our human awareness, one wherein, if we dig just a little deeper into it, there might well be far reaching implications on the subject of who and what we really are and some of the yet unknown things we are able do with our consciousness.

Basically we are not really that much different from other mammals and creatures. Beyond our ability to talk, the thing that makes human beings really stand out is our apparent ability to create a conceptual image of the world and then relate to that idea (or any idea apparently) to the exclusion of virtually everything and anything else. Thus, our densely populated human world is full of different cultures and beliefs, all competitively vying and clamouring for attention. So much so, that some suggest humanity has gradually become divorced from the underlying background reality that all other living creatures on this planet still have and retain an awareness of. Accordingly, human beings, via this ability, have created their very own multifaceted 'version' of reality, one that increasingly flies in the face of the way things are in reality for the rest of nature, to the point that most people these days generally feel that they lack a deeper connection to the rest of the universe, an idea that leaves them feeling somehow empty or incomplete and thus has people searching for some kind of deeper meaning to life, whether it be religion or philosophy. The standard social norm of having a good job, a nice home and family, doesn't always seem totally to fulfil that yearning need. I suppose this is precisely where religion and philosophy are supposed to come into the picture, except that those religions and philosophies themselves also often seem to fail us, in that almost all our religions only really succeed in distancing us even farther from nature instead of bringing us closer to it. Our religions comfort us by pertaining to answer all our questions, only they don't really answer them beyond telling us to behave ourselves in the meantime, while at the same time, rather frustratingly, just putting off the whole subject until after we die. As such they are more a way of 'explaining away' the mysteries of life rather than bringing us closer to them.

I suspect the simple truth is that there is probably no 'sense' (no meaning per se, or at least not a rational one) to life in quite the way we might want there to be; that while we are alive we can, of course, do all the usual things that the majority of people like to do, such as working and having homes and families. Nevertheless, we still have to understand that all these 'things' do not really constitute nor represent the 'meaning of life' in and of themselves. Yet in modern society that is exactly and precisely what people are encouraged to turn to for some sort of sense of completion and solace. The end result is that no one really knows what they are doing any more. More often than not, we merely bluff our way through life instead of consciously living it to the full in complete awareness of doing so.

What then is this 'fullness' we seek, where is this 'life more abundant' that everyone inwardly craves but can't really find? I don't have any definitive answers, although being a keen observer I do think I've managed to pick up a few clues here and there that might just well be of interest to those with similarly inquiring minds. For example, if there's such a thing as a meaning to life and we are part of it, then we really shouldn't have to look any further than into our own inner being in order to be able to understand it all, or at least our own part in it.

Perhaps by going along with the universe, instead of rebelling against it by indulging in all our own ideas that we project and superimpose upon the world instead of dealing with it the way it really is, we might just gain a few insights. Not because we have so cleverly figured it all out with our pencils and computers and such like, but because by going along with things sometimes you can also come to understand more of its true nature and that, although it may not be able to give you straight verbal answers, that doesn't mean you can't still learn something from observing the way it behaves and conducts itself with you and with everything else.

Maybe what we have to try and first understand and accept is that nature itself isn't intellectual and that, in the main, it has got to where it has today after billions of years of unfolding without the benefits of rational thinking and language to explain it; that although its purpose, its (and thus our) whole reason for being, is a totally silent one that requires no explanation to function, which doesn't mean we can't still learn to go along with it and pick up a few interesting and useful things about it and ourselves in the process. Nature is our friend. Nature doesn't lie. In other words, if we start off at home by looking a little more into our own nature and our own natural abilities, then later may come a view of the bigger picture in which we all naturally belong.

This is something that, for me, means examining this ability to lucid dream. Not that lucid dreaming is the only way to begin looking deeper into ourselves; far from it – it was simply this particular item of novel awareness that later became an in-road for putting together a rational explanation for our seemingly innate ability to lucid dream. I mean, it's phenomenal really, to be able to create a three-dimensional image in our minds and then inhabit such images by projecting ourselves into them in a totally realistic and utterly convincing manner that we then call having ordinary non-lucid dreams, or if you realise it's actually going on, lucid ones. If it was all on account of being limited to just ordinary random dreams alone I'd probably have to go along with the rationalists who suggest it's only the resting mind and brain on standby doing the housekeeping and getting itself ready for the following day's activities. However, that doesn't in any way explain how we can become wide awake in those dreams and wander round in them fully conscious, treating them as though they were another complete yet separate reality – a personal Holodeck effectively, in which you can play around as a nice little addition, perhaps, to an otherwise overcrowded and busy agenda, but not exactly something one could call an earth-shattering breakthrough. Interesting yes, earth-shattering no, unless these multi-layered dream realms could also be something to do with parallel worlds and/or dimensions, possibly even the gateway to them?

A possible proof of dream worlds being representative of the reality of other dimensions and parallel worlds would be if people could meet up with each other and communicate on those levels of awareness rather than being merely confined to the limitations of one's own imagination and the phantom images of other people. I have a sneaking suspicion that it can be done. The Australian Aborigines don't seem to have any problem accepting such a thing. I've certainly had some very odd experiences in that direction, things that make me question and ponder the possibility, but nothing so far that could possibly stand as representing any kind of definitive evidence of such a thing existing. If we can do it, then why is it so difficult to reproduce?

Maybe someone will get lucky one day and be able to tell us what we've all been doing wrong, but so far it just doesn't seem to work. I've certainly talked to quite a few people in my dreams, but if they're all really just figments of my own imagination then I guess I don't actually want to talk to them, except perhaps as their possibly being hidden aspects of myself. (Hey, Freud, bring it on!)

Even so, and even if that implies a more solitary journey into that of our own inner nature, then so be it. One's spirituality and/or inner nature might indeed just then be a strictly personal relationship that we all have in common with this big old world on whose back we've been hitching a ride. (I hesitate to say like fleas on a dog, but for some strange comical reason that's always the image I get.)

But I digress; basically I was trying to put it to you that the general nature of perception is, at its roots, dream-like and that this just might account for why we sometimes take our ordinary dreams for being unreal instead of recognising them for what they really are, i.e., altered states of awareness that we are compelled to enter into on a daily basis for the kind of energetic rejuvenation they afford, dreams in which one can be either awake or unconscious, albeit with the same result: we become refreshed.

From the multi-faceted point of view of WILDs, it turns out that lucid dreaming is the activation of only one possible state of altered awareness and the things you can do with it.

Another option is the waking state that everyone otherwise takes for granted but which may also be a kind of dream, perceptually speaking. Obviously, there's more to us than just those abilities alone, namely, that where there's one altered state of awareness that everyone can agree on, then it's reasonable to assume there are probably more.

So then we can either treat lucid dreaming as a thing in itself, the only goal of WILDs so to speak, or we can treat it as just one small part of a much larger, overall awareness that includes doing things 'like' lucid dreaming. This question doesn't even seem to arise or even present itself from the point of view of DILDs in which the exclusive objective is restricted to lucid dreaming.

Is there a philosophy to lucid dreaming? Is there something, a meaning behind it all? There undoubtedly is, albeit currently hidden from view, and discovering, unravelling and understanding that philosophy is obviously going to take time and experience, not because it's particularly difficult but because it's a whole new field of endeavour containing as yet unrealised reference points. The implications and ramifications of this hypothesis, I'm waging, could well be far-reaching, if not immense, in terms of obtaining a greater understanding of ourselves and the nature of the world around us.

Frequently Asked Questions

What is lucid dreaming?

Lucid dreaming means becoming aware that you are dreaming. There are, however, different degrees of lucidity that can be experienced. When lucidity is full, you are completely aware that everything experienced in the dream is occurring only in your mind; that you are safe and asleep in your bed and will awaken later. Full lucidity also means that you have full access to your waking memories, concepts and ideas. Whereas with semi-lucidity, you will be only aware to certain degrees that you are dreaming, enough perhaps to alter the things you are doing, but maybe not enough to fully understand and remember that other people in the dream are only dream images, or that you can suffer no physical harm and that you are at home in bed.

How easy is it to lucid dream?

Depending on the method employed, it can be very easy to have incredible lucid dreams within a relatively short period of time. The standard method of 'Dream-Induced Lucid Dreaming' (DILD) takes a frustratingly long time to accomplish. However, using the Waking-Induced Lucid Dreaming (WILD) method quite profound perceptual experiences can be achieved from the outset.

Is lucid dreaming the same as dream control?

The amount of control you experience and can exert over a given dream is in direct proportion to the degree of lucidity you are experiencing. With DILDs that lucidity can vary to an enormous degree from session to session. With WILDs *full* lucidity is usually one of the most remarkable features of the dream itself.

Why have lucid dreams?

There are many reasons why a person may want to experience lucid dreaming, for example:
- To have a fun and energising experience;
- To explore elements of your imagination and sensations that are not possible in your waking life, such as flying;
- To face, and learn to deal with, real fears from your waking life, such as phobias;
- To rehearse for real life events;
- To discover solutions to problems that are difficult to solve in conscious mind;
- For the purposes of self-healing or to promote better health
- To experience freedom of movement if this is normally restricted in your waking life;
- Spiritual fulfilment and to re-examine your perspective on life and living.

Can lucid dreaming be dangerous?

No! The point being that the whole thing is just a vivid dream that you will shortly wake up from no matter what happens in the dream itself. For example, someone I know reported being suddenly confronted by a huge tiger (tiger? tiger! Lol) but again, kept their cool and simple turned around and left the room, leaving the tiger behind. Pretty neat solution huh?

Can everyone learn to have lucid dreams?

Yes! With WILDs anyone and everyone can do it. Lucid dreaming is an innate ability that all human beings share in common. All it takes being determination and perseverance.

How do I learn to have lucid dreams?

The first step is to open oneself to the idea that it's possible to be able to do so. Then follow the techniques outlined in this book to achieve your first lucid dreaming experience.

Why is recalling dreams so difficult?

Being awake in the waking world is a wholly different state of awareness to that of being awake in a dream and each requires different handling. This only becomes noticeable once someone learns to lucid dream due to not having anything beforehand to compare one's normal waking awareness to. The difference between them is so wide that an obscuring blanket seemingly exists between them. This is the reason that upon waking, many people, although feeling they have dreamed, typically cannot remember them. The natural result of this is to completely forget them unless a memory is jogged by some, usually insignificant event.

What is reality testing?

Reality testing is a procedure used with the DILD form of lucid dreaming. It is a way of pre-programming oneself to ask at different points in time 'Am I dreaming or not?' to discover if you are, in fact, dreaming.

What are dream signs and MILDs

Mnemonic Induction of Lucid Dreams (MILDs) is a way of pre-programming oneself to observe certain inconsistencies in one's perception, for example, by chanting a mantra as you fall asleep to remind you to be awake in your dreams.

How quickly can I learn to lucid dream?

Using the WILD method as outlined in this book, you can learn to have lucid dreams, on demand, relatively quickly. Within a month or less, easily!

What technology is available to assist lucid dreaming?

All the technology that currently purports to assist with lucid dreaming is strictly only for use with the DILD method. None of which is required (or even necessary) with WILDs. Flashing face masks, ambient sounds plus goodness knows what, only exist in the first place to 'remind' you that you're dreaming, something that WILDs makes completely redundant. Don't bother with them.

Should I use nutritional supplements to stimulate lucid dreaming?

No! Additional supplements are not necessary and will not help you to have lucid dreams apart from maybe having a placebo effect; there is no 'magic pill'. You can rest assured that your body and brain already has all the possible chemicals it ever needs to do lucid dreaming well. An averagely healthy brain needs nothing more.

How can I prevent myself waking up every time I become lucid?

The first thing to do is to remain calm. Being lucid in a dream is very exciting, but getting too excited can and will awaken you from it. Therefore an emotional balance has to be quickly learned and struck between enjoying your lucid dream to its fullest, while at the same time not allowing yourself to become too carried-away by the sheer excitement of it.

What are false awakenings?

A false awakening is the experience of having a lucid dream, or even just an ordinary dream, and thinking that you've woken up for real in your own house only to discover moments later when you try to switch on the light or the coffee pot, that you are, in fact, still asleep and dreaming.

How can I experience flying in dreaming?

In a dream anything is possible and flying is no exception. You'll have to experiment a bit, but generally, when you want to fly in your dreams simply will yourself up into the air. Start off small, levitating by say, maybe only few centimetres at a time or so and progress from there. Increased experience quickly brings its own rewards and flying in dreaming rapidly becomes easy, if not completely standard.

Can I become stuck in a lucid dream?

No! It's only a dream and as long as you don't panic at all there's no reason why any situation cannot be resolved.

For example, someone I know deliberately dreamed that they had gone into outer space and was looking at the Earth from a great height. Suddenly, the Earth was gone and they found themselves totally alone surrounded only by stars and the utter blackness of space! Being an experienced dreamer, however, they didn't panic but calmly closed their eyes and visualised a scene here on Earth and when they opened their eyes again they were back on Earth and carried on. Cool!

Are my dreams psychic?

If you mean 'of the psyche' (the mind) then yes they are. Totally. Lucid dreams are purely a product of the mind. If you instead mean can they be used to predict the future? Then probably not. If you mean can I be psychic *within* a dream? Then yes! Levitation (flying), moving objects around in a dream by thought alone (psychokinesis), creating objects and even people (creativity) plus many more, are all available to the dreamer. But only within a dream.

Can I communicate with my subconscious in a lucid dream?

Apparently so! Just ask questions out loud and see what happens. You may be surprised by the results! For example, misplaced items in the waking world can often be recovered by enquiring of their whereabouts in dreaming. Subconsciously, you probably know exactly where you left them and such hidden memories can easily be accessed via dreaming. Albert Einstein reputedly even solved complex mathematical problems in his dreams!

If I die in a dream will I die in reality?

No! This really is an old wives' tale! Usually, if and/or when you *maybe* dream of dying or being killed (not everyone does but it's happened to me several times) you usually just wake up in your bed rather abruptly albeit maybe feeling a bit shocked for the experience, heh. Don't worry about it. It's not real.

What are out-of-body experiences (OBEs)?

An out-of-body experience (OBE) is the feeling of floating or existing outside of the physical body and is similar, perhaps, to Astral projection, which many people attest to experiencing. This is something completely different to lucid dreaming, although at times it does indeed feel like you have been from your body in the sense that, with WILDs, you can still feel your body lying down in bed whilst still dreaming.

OBEs themselves may or may not actually exist and only exist in dreams. But currently no one can yet say for certain if this is really true or not, so the whole subject of the *reality* of OBEs remains open to conjecture.

Does lucid dreaming expand the mind?

Yes! Being unconscious in our dreams mirrors just how unconscious and asleep we are in our waking lives, which from a waking point of view is an irremediable situation *per se*. One avenue for redemption remains, however, in that with awareness it's always a two-way street because, change one and you effectively change the other!

The end result (of lucid dreaming) is to make people more thoughtful and aware of their waking surroundings and the lives they're living. This is because becoming more lucid and aware in dreams automatically carries over into becoming more lucid and aware during waking, something which ultimately equates with a general increase in awareness overall.

So yes, lucid dreaming *does* genuinely expand the mind!

PART 4 – RESOURCES

Recommended Reading

Hervey de Saint-Denys, Marie-Jean-Léon, *Dreams and How to Guide Them*, editor Morton Schatzman M.D., London: Duckworth, 1982.

Godwin, Malcolm, *The Lucid Dreamer: A Waking Guide for the Traveler Between Worlds*, Simon & Schuster, 1994.

Green, Celia E., *Lucid Dreams*, London: Hamish Hamilton, 1968.

LaBerge, Stephen, Lucid Dreaming: A Concise Guide to Awakening in Your Dreams and in Your Life, Sounds True Inc, 2009.

LaBerge, Stephen, and Rheingold, Howard, *Exploring the World of Lucid Dreaming*, Ballantine, 1990.

Van de Castle, Robert L., *Our Dreaming Mind*, Ballantine, 1994.

Other Resources

The best place for resources is undoubtedly online. Surfing the internet should be more than enough to completely familiarise you with all the general workings of lucid dreaming one could need to know. Although, I stress that you should add the term WILD to any searches lest all the material you find will only be about those difficult DILDs.

Typing something like: 'lucid+dreams+wild' (including the quotes) into your favourite search engine, will undoubtedly throw out some choice articles, leaving '+wilds' off the end if you'd like more information on DILDs. You could also try adding 'hypnagogia' to maybe expand that list.

However, the above is a short list of current books that I recommend reading, although any similar search on somewhere like Amazon will very quickly put you in touch with all the authors to be found on the subject. Just remember that most of that written material is unfortunately almost exclusively about the DILDs method.

Glossary of Lucid Dreaming Terms

Cycle Adjustment Technique – Adjusting one's sleep cycles to increase the likelihood of having a lucid dream.
DILD – Dream-Induced Lucid Dream. A lucid dream that begins during a 'normal', non-lucid dream.
Dream character – Any character inside one's dream. Some believe they are real people or even spirit guides, others that they're merely products of the dreaming mind.
Dream recall – The ability to remember details of one's dreams when awake.
Dream result – Result from a reality check that indicates that one is dreaming; e.g., breathing through the nose while pinching the nostrils.
Dreamscape – The scenery and landscape of your dreams.
EILD – Erotically-Induced Lucid Dream. A lucid dream that includes sexual activity.
Hypnagogic images – The images and sounds that you typically perceive when you're falling asleep.
Lucid dream – A dream in which you are aware that you are dreaming.
LILD – Lucid Induction of Lucid Dreams –A technique in which you do something in a lucid dream that will remind you that you're dreaming in your next dream.
MILD – Mnemonic Induction of Lucid Dreams. A technique in which you mentally repeat to yourself, as you fall asleep, one's future intention to realise that you're dreaming.
Oneironaut – A skilled lucid dreamer.
Phosphenes – Patches of colour (usually red or blue) that you can see while your eyes are closed.

Reality check – A simple method of determining if one is dreaming or not; e.g., learning to repeatedly ask oneself if one is dreaming or not.

Real-life result – A reality check result that indicates you are not dreaming; e.g., being 'unable' to will oneself to fly.

REM – Rapid Eye Movement. The stage of sleep in which one's most vivid dreams occur.

SP – Sleep paralysis. The body's natural manner of paralysing your body while asleep.

VILD – Visual Induction of Lucid Dreams. A technique in which you incubate a dream that reminds you to do a reality check.

Vivid dream – A dream with notably higher levels of detail.

WBTB – Wake-Back-To-Bed. A technique in which you wake up for a while after a few hours of sleep and then go back to sleep again.

WILD – Waking-Induced Lucid Dream. A lucid dream engendered by consciously falling asleep.

Acknowledgements

Charles Alvin White (Pogo); a street-savvy Brixton hustler and wise man from Kingston, Jamaica, who, for some reason known only to him, took a shy and timid young white guy under his wing and showed him the ropes and London street-smarts by taking him around and introducing him to the way things really *are*.

Thank you Pogo, for the education, sheer patience and understanding you displayed in building my confidence and giving me a clear sense of direction, plus many other useful things besides! I am forever in your debt.

Buddha Maitreya, Purelands, Lincoln, UK; a Japanese Zen Master who cured my young man's over-sensitivity and paranoia, who taught me meditation and gave me genuine peace of mind among many other good things and useful abilities, things that have stood me in good stead even to this day! Thank you kind and helpful friend.

David Ian Gray; unknown genius and highly educated/evolved man from the streets of Brixton. A painter and decorator by trade and probably the wisest person it's ever been my privilege to know. The finest mentor anyone could ever hope to have and from whom I learned about literature, history and philosophy, plus a myriad of other things about life, the universe and everything – too much to mention. Thank you 'Digger' for all that work you so unselfishly and humbly imparted, and for which I can never thank you enough. You the man!

To all the 'dudes' and 'dude-esses' of the (unmoderated): Alt.Dreams.Castaneda online Usenet Newsgroup where I first learned to lucid dream and use the nickname 'slider'. All of whom it has been my privilege to associate and (heh) 'exchange messages' with for nigh on eighteen years at the time of writing.

You may, or may not, have been a bit 'off the wall' in your initial beliefs and participation surrounding the works of writer Carlos Castaneda and the movement he created with such gusto, but nevertheless remain some of *the* most honest, intelligent and affable people one could ever hope to meet and interact with online.

I don't know about Castaneda (as I never personally met him) – but all you guys were, and are, as sharp as razors!

With particular thanks to 'CRSDS' (Chris) whom I originally met online and was invited to ADC by, 'Jeremy' (Dave), 'Thang', 'Dan', 'Eldon' (Vinny), 'Andy', 'Temporal', 'Randy', 'Ann' and 'Unc' – plus a whole host of oh so many others! Thank you. It's all been most educational and highly enjoyable!

Dr. Peter J. Newey PhD., A lifelong friend. Thank you, Pete, for *being* a friend and for encouraging and aiding me to turn a pile of messy, unstructured notes into something resembling a book to work with. You are literally *the* most academically educated person I have ever met and has been my privilege to know! I sincerely thank you indeed for your invaluable assistance in preparing me, and this book, for publication! Thank you always.

Kim Kimber BA (Hons) English and History, Advanced Professional Member of the SfEP (www.kimkimber.co.uk).

Thank you, Kim, for your wonderful editing skills and immensely encouraging assistance in bringing a new author right through to their difficult first publication. Your writing and editing abilities are truly amazing! And I can quite honestly say that I couldn't have possibly done it without you! I can never thank you enough.

Kind thanks are also tendered to Carmen Hernandez Pinzon (current copyright holder) and grandniece of Juan Ramón Jiménez; for the use of *Hora Inmensa* at the end of this work.

And to everyone else who knows me!
Thank you all.

Hora Inmensa

Only a bell and a bird break the stillness...
It seems that the two talk with the setting sun.
Golden colored silence, the afternoon is made of crystals.
A roving purity sways the cool trees,
And beyond all that,
A transparent river dreams that trampling over pearls
It breaks loose
And flows into infinity.

~ Juan Ramón Jímenez

Printed in Great Britain
by Amazon